PEARL HARBOR

Roosevelt and the Coming of the War

Revised Edition

Problems in American Civilization

UNDER THE EDITORIAL DIRECTION OF George Rogers Taylor

PEARL HARBOR
Roosevelt and the Coming of the War

Revised Edition

EDITED WITH AN INTRODUCTION BY
George M. Waller

BUTLER UNIVERSITY

Problems in American Civilization

D. C. HEATH AND COMPANY: Boston

ENGLEWOOD · CHICAGO · DALLAS · SAN FRANCISCO · ATLANTA · LONDON · TORONTO

INTRODUCTION

OVER two decades have passed since December 7, 1941, that "day of infamy" on which Japanese bombers and submarines surprised the United States at Pearl Harbor and inflicted upon this nation the worst military defeat in its history. Almost immediately the question was asked: "How could it have happened?" The question was asked and answered (a hundred different ways) with passion. To know what happened at Pearl Harbor, *and why,* is to know American foreign policy in the 1930's, for the controversy that raged over the responsibility for the disaster of December 7th was a continuation of the debate that had raged, between interventionists and isolationists, all through the 1930's.

The disputants in the "great debate" over involvement in the war closed ranks after Pearl Harbor, as the prewar disputants have characteristically closed ranks in our other wars, in order to present a united front to the Axis powers. Once the war had ended, historians, political leaders, editorial writers and others reopened the debate, reviewed the causes of the war (in the bright light of historical hindsight) and revised previous judgments. Such a reassessment, technically known as "revisionism," is also characteristic; it is both the attempt of students of history to put the past crisis into perspective and the sign of a reemergence of those passionate partisanships that had remained—more or less—submerged during the course of the war.

Thus, after World War II some who were opposed to intervention sought to find justification for their earlier argument that America should have pursued a course that kept it clear of the warring powers of Europe and Asia. Others see more clearly alternatives that were not apparent at the time. And those who supported American involvement in the world crisis defend, of course, the policies that ultimately led to war.

Discussion centers on two principal matters. The more important is the question of how and why we entered World War II. Was President Franklin D. Roosevelt personally responsible for plunging us into an unnecessary war? Did he do all he could to avoid or postpone war, or did he actually seek to involve the country? Could the United States wisely have avoided war by pursuing a different policy? If so, what would have been the chief characteristics of such a policy?

Within this general question is a particular one: Who was responsible for the surprise and unpreparedness of our forces when war actually came? If Roosevelt *had* sought the war, why had he not done more to alert our forces to the nature of the danger? How much intelligence information was available and how effectively was it acted on? Was it mere incompetence, either at the top, in Washington, or in the field, at Pearl Harbor? Who, in the chain of command that ran from the President and his top Cabinet advisers in Washington down to those on the decks of ships at anchor, was to blame for permitting the Japanese to catch us by surprise?

The arguments having to do with these questions, as readers of the following selections will discover, are compounded of various beliefs and allegations, often mutually contradictory. Roosevelt is accused by his enemies of preparing for war and by his friends of reluctance and delay in meeting the inevitable. His detractors charge him with leading the country into war while professing a policy of peace; turning to the Far East to "maneuver" Japan into striking its blow when he found isolationist opposition too strong to permit him to bring the United States into war on the side of embattled Britain.

Some supporters of the President find extenuation for his deception in the short-sighted opposition of isolationists who stood ready to block measures deemed essential to the country's security. Others insist that Roosevelt had no desire to lead the United States into war and that his policies were those of collective security, the only course open to a nation professing adherence to principles of morality and international law. If this policy ultimately failed to avoid war, it was because the course of the totalitarian powers finally left no alternative that would not be at the same time a shameful abandonment of American principles and the exposure of the nation to extreme peril.

With the passage of years, division of opinion occurs even more broadly. Disillusionment over the grave problems left by the war led some historians to raise the question of "morality vs. realism" in foreign policy, and to ask whether a "hard" policy to compel Japanese adherence to principles of international law was either moral or realistic when it led to war and the problems of the postwar world. For these critics the situation faced by the United States in these years of Cold War is evidence that the war against Germany and Japan should have been avoided. Judged by what followed, intervention in the name of international law or moral principles strikes them as hypocritical or unrealistic.

A major issue emerging from the controversy involves conflicting judgments on the nature of the political structure of the world, especially the Far East and the forces that led to Hitler's rise and to Japan's aggression. What dangers existed in this aggression for the United States? What commitments had we to nations threatened by aggressors? Did we do enough to understand the problems of those we opposed? Did not our role in the war destroy the alignment of powers and leave us worse problems in foreign policy? Roosevelt's adherents find this wisdom of hindsight insufficient and charge their opponents with distorting the picture, ignoring the threat of totalitarianism on the Right, along with Japan's attachment to the Axis powers, in their concern for the shadow of a later powerful Communism.

Hostility toward the strong executive leadership of "that man in the White House" led Roosevelt's critics to charge him with an act of criminal negligence for failure to keep the Pacific outposts better informed about the developing crisis. He must bear the blame, in their eyes, both for the coming of the war and for the disastrous surprise at Pearl Harbor. Others favorable to Roosevelt's leadership exonerated Roosevelt and found the island commanders or their staffs guilty or incompetent.

The debate which the student will find in the following pages is a continuing one. For the surprise at Pearl Harbor, other evidence may yet be forthcoming. New disclosures are hinted at from time to time and some of the people involved remain to be heard from. But for the American policies that led to the coming of the war, whether they were all they should or could have been, it is safe to say that the facts necessary to make a judgment are at hand and each of us must form his own opinions. They will remain a matter of dispute because persons with varying interests and philosophies interpret the facts in different ways and come to divergent conclusions.

The discussion is a matter of importance because with world power has come world responsibility. The foreign policy of the United States, long little more than a by-product of domestic issues, is now a central factor in the economics and politics of much of the world. The decisions made by Franklin Roosevelt affected every American citizen; the decisions made by his successors affect America's friends from Tokyo to West Berlin, and America's foes from Peking to whatever highway or hamlet or barbed-wire fence next becomes the focus of attention for those of us who participate, willing or not, in the crisis of the postwar world.

CONTENTS

CHRONOLOGY

1931	Japan invades Manchuria
1931	Hoover's Secretary of State announces the *Stimson Doctrine*
1933	Japan leaves the League of Nations
1935	Italy attacks Ethiopia
1936	Spanish Civil War; Germany reoccupies the Rhineland
1937	Japan opens undeclared war on China
1935–37	U. S. passes Neutrality Acts
1937	Roosevelt's *Quarantine Speech*
1938	Hitler takes Austria; British and French sign the *Munich Pact* "appeasing" Hitler
March, 1939	Hitler takes Czechoslovakia; Mussolini invades Albania
July, 1939	U. S. gives Japan notice of abrogation of reciprocal trade treaties
August, 1939	Germany and Russia sign nonaggression pact
September 3, 1939	WAR: Hitler invades Poland; Britain and France declare war on Germany
November, 1939	U. S. Congress repeals arms embargo, puts trade with belligerents on "cash and carry" basis
April–June, 1940	*Blitzkrieg:* Fall of Denmark, Norway, The Netherlands, Belgium, France
September, 1940	Destroyer-Bases Agreement
September, 1940	Congress passes Selective Service Act, by one-vote margin
November, 1940	Roosevelt re-elected for third term
January–March, 1941	Joint military staff talks, U. S. and Britain
March, 1941	Lend-Lease Act
March, 1941	Hull and Nomura begin talks in Washington
April, 1941	Roosevelt orders U. S. Navy to patrol in Western Atlantic
June, 1941	Hitler attacks Russia
July, 1941	U. S. occupies Iceland bases
July, 1941	Japanese Imperial Conference determines to continue policy in Asia
July 24, 1941	Japan moves into Indo-China
July 26, 1941	U. S. freezes Japanese assets
August 9–14, 1941	Atlantic Conference: Roosevelt and Churchill meet at Argentia
August 17, 1941	U. S. warning to Japan
August–September, 1941	Prime Minister Konoye requests meeting with Roosevelt
September–October, 1941	U. S. destroyers attacked in Atlantic
September 6, 1941	Konoye offers proposals to U. S.
October 2, 1941	U. S. note rejecting Konoye's proposals and deferring proposed meeting
October 17, 1941	Konoye Cabinet falls; Tojo becomes Prime Minister
November 7, 1941	U. S. rejects Japanese Imperial Conference's "Proposal A"
November 17, 1941	Kurusu arrives in Washington to join Nomura
November 20, 1941	U. S. rejects Japanese "Proposal B"

November 22–26, 1941   Hull weighs idea of a "modus vivendi," and rejects it

November 26, 1941   U. S. offers comprehensive proposal to Japan

November 27, 1941   U. S. Army and Navy send war warnings to Hawaii, Philippines, Guam, and other outposts

December 5–6, 1941   Japanese destroying codes and preparing to close embassy. Troop movements south from Indo-China

December 6, 1941   Roosevelt sends personal plea to Japanese Emperor

December 6, 1941   U. S. begins interception of fourteen-part Japanese message rejecting November 26 offer

December 7, 1941   1:50 P.M.: Washington learns of Pearl Harbor attack

THE CLASH OF ISSUES

Roosevelt's opponents maintain:

... America was stealthily maneuvered into war behind the backs and without the knowledge of the elected representatives of the American people. . . . Like the Roman god Janus, Roosevelt in the prewar period had two faces. For the American people, for the public record, there was the face of bland assurance that his first concern was to keep the country out of war. But in more intimate surroundings the Chief Executive often assumed that America was already involved in war. . . . Seldom if ever in American history was there such a gulf between appearances and realities, between Presidential words and Presidential deeds.

WILLIAM HENRY CHAMBERLIN

... Roosevelt and Hull knew from the cracked Japanese code that the Japanese peace offers were sincere and reasonable, but, nevertheless, rebuffed them and provoked the Japanese attack on Pearl Harbor.

HARRY ELMER BARNES

... no amount of excuses will palliate the conduct of President Roosevelt and his advisers. The offense of which they stand convicted is not failure to discharge their responsibilities, but calculated refusal to do so. They failed — with calculation — to keep the United States out of war and to avoid a clash with Japan. . . . The "warnings" they sent to Hawaii failed — and were so phrased and so handled as to insure failure.

GEORGE MORGENSTERN

Roosevelt himself sought methods short of war by which the nation's security could be safeguarded:

If Great Britain goes down, the Axis powers will control the continents of Europe, Asia, Africa, Australia and the high seas — and they will be in a position to bring enormous military and naval resources against this hemisphere. . . . There is far less chance of the United States getting into the war if we do all we can now to support the nations defending themselves against the Axis. . . .

Fireside Chat, December 29, 1940

His supporters conclude:

On the American side the perspective is unclouded. This government hoped, against its better judgment, for a comprehensive settlement of the Far Eastern problems, and, failing that, nursed a more limited and pragmatic hope that hostilities might be staved off for as long as the Japanese were willing to talk.

FORREST DAVIS and ERNEST K. LINDLEY

And a State Department expert on the Far East writes:

The Japanese were not offering to negotiate a reasonable settlement by processes of agreement; they were presenting demands, to be accepted or rejected. The United States had only two choices: either to yield to the Japanese demands and sacrifice principles and security, or to decline to yield and take the consequences.

JOSEPH W. BALLANTINE

William Henry Chamberlin:

ROOSEVELT MANEUVERS AMERICA INTO WAR

William Henry Chamberlin is a well-known author and lecturer, editorial writer for the Wall Street Journal; *for over ten years he served as Moscow correspondent for the* Christian Science Monitor. *In the lead selection below, from his work* America's Second Crusade, *he charges the President and his advisers with leading the country into war while professing a policy of peace. Roosevelt, Chamberlin maintains, was irrevocably committing America to the cause of the anti-Axis powers while insisting that his policy was designed to avoid war. When he found isolationist opposition too strong, he turned to the Far East and "maneuvered" Japan into striking the blow that would accomplish his purpose. In the pungent words of Clare Booth Luce, "He lied the American people into war because he could not lead them into it."*

THE momentous issue of deliberate involvement in the European war might well have been submitted to a referendum of the American people in the presidential election of 1940. The majority of the Republicans in both houses of Congress before and after this election systematically voted against measures calculated to bring about this involvement.

Had Roosevelt frankly presented to the voters the program which he actually carried out in 1941 (lend-lease, convoys, undeclared shooting war in the Atlantic, commercial blockade of Japan) and had Roosevelt's opponent been a sincerely noninterventionist Republican a very interesting discussion would certainly have ensued. The verdict of the people would then have given a clear mandate either to go into the war frankly and vigorously or to stay out of it, except in the event of direct attack.

But neither of the leading candidates in the 1940 election made a candid statement of his position on the most important issue confronting the American people. A comparison of Roosevelt's words before the election and of his deeds after the election fully substantiates the tart comment of Clare Booth Luce: "He lied the American people into war because he could not lead them into it."

And by an unfortunate accident of American politics the Republican nomination did not go to a man who shared the viewpoint of the majority of Republican members of Congress. The candidate was Wendell Willkie, a newcomer in politics, a man who in the preceding autumn had volunteered to raise money for interventionist purposes.

The result was that the very large number of American voters who wanted to stay out of the war were, for all practical purposes, disfranchised. The campaign was an amazing exhibition of double talk. Roosevelt and Willkie vied with each

Reprinted by permission from *America's Second Crusade* by William Henry Chamberlin (Chicago: Henry Regnery Company), copyright 1950, excerpted material from pages 120–147.

other in making the most sweeping promises to keep the country at peace. The frequency and forcefulness of these pledges mounted to a crescendo as the election day approached. This was a significant straw in the wind, indicating how the majority of voters in both parties felt on the issue. There were evidently few votes to be won and many to be lost by a frank call to arms.

Both platforms contained antiwar commitments. The Democratic read: "We will not participate in foreign wars and we will not send our army, naval or air forces to fight in foreign lands outside the Americas, except in case of attack."

The equivalent Republican statement was more concise: "The Republican Party is firmly opposed to involving this nation in foreign wars."

Willkie said in Chicago on September 13: "If you elect me President, I will never send an American boy to fight in a European war."

He told his audience in Cleveland on October 2: "I am for keeping out of war. I am for peace for America."

He declared in Philadelphia on October 4: "We must stop this drift toward war," and in a radio broadcast on October 8 he asserted: "We must keep out of war at all hazards." He told the voters of Boston on October 11: "Our boys shall stay out of European wars." On October 22 he offered the following explanation of the difference between his foreign policy and that of the Administration:

"One difference is my determination to stay out of war. I have a real fear that this Administration is heading for war, and I am against our going to war and will do all that I can to avoid it."

So Willkie, whose whole attitude after the election promoted the "drift toward war" which he condemned before the

votes were counted, tried to win as the champion of peace against war. But he could not outbid Roosevelt in promises on this issue. Between October 28 and November 3 the President gave repeated assurances that he would not lead the country into any foreign wars. As his admirer, Robert E. Sherwood, says:

That Madison Square Garden speech (on October 28) was one of the most equivocal of Roosevelt's career. . . . Here Roosevelt went to the length or depth of taking credit for the Neutrality Law and other measures which he had thoroughly disapproved and had fought to repeal and had contrived by all possible means to circumvent. While boasting of the Neutrality Law as part of the Administration record, he deliberately neglected to make any mention of his own Quarantine Speech.[1]

Two days later, in Boston, Roosevelt went even further. "Fear-of-war hysteria," in Sherwood's phrase, seemed to be growing. Telegrams poured in from Democratic leaders, urging the President to make stronger and more specific antiwar pledges. The election, according to these telegrams, hung in the balance. Henri IV thought Paris was worth a Mass. Roosevelt apparently believed that another term of power was worth promises which would soon be disregarded, which could be broken without incurring legal liability. At the urging of Sherwood[2] he decided to strengthen his pledge with the words "again and again and again." And the rich, soothing voice poured out to the audience at Boston the following reassurance:

While I am talking to you mothers and fathers, I give you one more assurance.

[1] *Roosevelt and Hopkins* (New York, Harper, 1948), p. 189.
[2] *Ibid.*, p. 191.

I have said this before, but I shall say it again and again and again.

Your boys are not going to be sent into any foreign wars.

On November 2 Roosevelt promised: "Your President says this nation is not going to war."

On November 3 he added: "The first purpose of our foreign policy is to keep our country out of war."[3]

No isolationist could have offered more sweeping and categorical pledges. How these pledges were observed will be the subject of the next two chapters. Professor Thomas A. Bailey, a sympathizer with Roosevelt's foreign policy, admits that the President's tactics were disingenuous, but offers an apology in the following passage:

Franklin Roosevelt repeatedly deceived the American people during the period before Pearl Harbor. . . . He was like the physician who must tell the patient lies for the patient's own good. . . . The country was overwhelmingly non-interventionist to the very day of Pearl Harbor, and an overt attempt to lead the people into war would have resulted in certain failure and an almost certain ousting of Roosevelt in 1940, with a consequent defeat of his ultimate aims.[4]

Professor Bailey offers the following somewhat Machiavellian conception as to how democracy should work.

A president who cannot entrust the people with the truth betrays a certain lack of faith in the basic tenets of democracy. But because the masses are notoriously shortsighted and generally cannot see danger until it is at their throats our statesmen are forced to deceive them into an awareness of their own

long run interests. This is clearly what Roosevelt had to do, and who shall say that posterity will not thank him for it?

That Roosevelt resorted to habitual deception of the American people both before and after the election of 1940 is not open to serious question. That such deception, on an issue which was literally a matter of life and death for many American citizens, savors of personal dictatorship rather than of democracy, responsive to the popular will, also seems obvious.

Whether Roosevelt's deception was justified is open to debate. This is a question which everyone must answer on the basis of what America's Second Crusade cost, what it accomplished, what kind of world emerged from it, and how real was the danger against which it was undertaken.

Road to War: The Atlantic

Roosevelt was elected President for a third term by the votes of isolationists who trusted his dozen or more specific pledges to stay out of war and of interventionists who did not believe he meant what he said. The latter had far more reason for satisfaction. Once assured of four more years in the White House, Roosevelt set the ship of state on a much more militant course. But the double talk, the carrying out of steps which logically pointed to full belligerence to an accompaniment of soothing "no war" assurances, continued almost until Pearl Harbor. . . .

Immediately after the election there was a political lull. Roosevelt departed on December 2 on a Caribbean cruise with Harry Hopkins as his only guest. The President was apparently mainly concerned with rest and recreation. But on this cruise he received a very important letter from Winston Churchill. In

[3] For a complete survey of the antiwar professions of Roosevelt and Willkie, see Charles A. Beard, *American Foreign Policy, 1932–1940* (Yale University Press, 1946), pp. 265–323.
[4] Thomas A. Bailey, *The Man in the Street* (New York, Macmillan, 1948), pp. 11–13.

this communication, dated December 8, one finds the final inspiration for the lend-lease idea.

Churchill emphasized two points: the serious threat of the submarine war and the approaching exhaustion of Britain's financial assets. He suggested that America should protect its shipments to Britain with warships. Realizing that this was probably too much to expect, he suggested, as an alternative, "the gift, loan or supply of a large number of American vessels of war." Another proposal, which was soon to bear fruit, was that the United States Navy should "extend its sea control of the American side of the Atlantic."

Churchill warned that the moment was approaching "when we shall no longer be able to pay cash for shipping and other supplies." After receiving this letter Roosevelt, according to Hopkins, came out one evening with the whole lend-lease scheme, the delivery of munitions and supplies free of charge to Great Britain and the other anti-Axis belligerents. "He didn't seem to have any clear idea how it could be done legally," Hopkins observes. "But there wasn't a doubt in his mind that he would find a way to do it."

After returning to Washington Roosevelt outlined the principle of lend-lease at a press conference. He used as an illustration the case of a man lending his garden hose to a neighbor whose house was on fire.

In the course of his "fireside" chat to the American people on December 29 the President painted a dire picture of the peril that was supposedly hanging over the Western Hemisphere.

Never since Jamestown and Plymouth Rock has American civilization been in such danger as now. . . . If Great Britain goes down, the Axis powers will control the continents of Europe, Asia, Africa, Australia and the high seas—and they will be in a position to bring enormous military and naval resources against this hemisphere. It is no exaggeration to say that all of us in the Americas would be living at the point of a gun—a gun loaded with explosive bullets, economic as well as military.

Yet along with this melodramatic scare note, which was to be struck again and again during 1941, there were soothing assurances that the United States would not get into the war.

There is far less chance of the United States getting into the war if we do all we can now to support the nations defending themselves against the Axis. . . . You can therefore nail any talk about sending armies to Europe as deliberate untruth. . . . We must be the arsenal of democracy.

Roosevelt outlined the plan for lend-lease aid to the anti-Axis powers in his message to Congress of January 6, 1941. This was the longest single stride on the road to war. For it is a long-recognized principle of international law that it is an act of war for a neutral government (as distinguished from private firms or agencies) to supply arms, munitions, and implements of war to a belligerent.

The United States had demanded and obtained heavy damages, by decision of a court of arbitration, from Great Britain because the British Government did not prevent the escape from a British port of the cruiser *Alabama*, built for the Confederacy, which subsequently preyed upon United States shipping. But Roosevelt brushed off objections based on international law with the off-the-cuff declaration:

"Such aid is not an act of war, even if a dictator should unilaterally proclaim it so to be."

The bill envisaged enormous and undefined expenditures and conferred vast and unprecedented discretionary powers upon the President. Its terms were to be effective "notwithstanding the provisions of any other law." But Roosevelt gave specific assurances that neither the Johnson Act, barring loans to countries in default on earlier obligations to the United States, nor the Neutrality Act, forbidding loans to belligerents, would be repealed.

Here was surely legal confusion heavily compounded. It was obvious that if the lend-lease bill should become law, the United States would have departed much farther from neutrality than Wilson had gone before America formally entered the First World War. Yet legislation enacted on the basis of America's experience in 1917, designed to keep the country out of war by foregoing neutral rights which Wilson had upheld, was left on the statute books. It was all very confusing; and confusion of public opinion was what Roosevelt needed gradually to steer America into undeclared hostilities while professing devotion to peace. . . .

In retrospect the adoption of the Lend-Lease Act seems to be the most decisive of the series of moves which put America into an undeclared war in the Atlantic months before Japan struck at Pearl Harbor. This measure marked the end of any pretense of neutrality. It underwrote the unconditional victory of Britain with America's industrial power and natural resources. It opened up the immediate prospect of an appeal for naval action to insure that the munitions and supplies procured under lend-lease would reach England in spite of the submarine blockade. While Congress and the American people were being officially assured that lend-lease was not a move toward war, Roosevelt's personal envoy, Harry Hopkins, was giving Churchill the following categorical pledge of all-out American aid in January 1941: "The President is

determined that we shall win the war together. Make no mistake about that."[5]

Yet this fateful measure was not frankly presented and advocated as equivalent to a state of limited belligerence. If one studies the record of the debates in House and Senate, one finds supporters of the bill employing this kind of reasoning:

"The present bill is a peace measure for our people."—Representative McCormack, of Massachusetts.

"In my judgment there is nothing in this bill which will hasten or accentuate our involvement in the war."—Representative Luther Johnson, of Texas.

"We believe that this measure offers the surest method by which we can avoid participation actively in this war and at the same time help those nations which are heroically grappling with a universal enemy and preserve the doctrines of our fathers and the aspirations of our own hearts."—Senator Alben Barkley, of Kentucky.

Leading Cabinet members and high military authorities testified on behalf of the bill and indulged in some very bad guessing. Frank Knox, Secretary of the Navy, predicted on January 17 a crisis within sixty days. On January 31 he forecast a great air blitz on Britain and the use of poison gas within sixty or ninety days. Stimson saw great danger of an airborne invasion and General Marshall predicted an attack on Great Britain in the spring. It is interesting to note that Churchill's authoritative memoirs do not bear out the alarmist arguments which were employed to push through the lend-lease bill. Describing the situation at the beginning of 1941, he points out in detail how British strength to resist a German invasion had immensely increased and states the following conclusion: "So long as there was no relaxation in vigilance or

[5] Winston Churchill, *The Grand Alliance* (Boston, Houghton Mifflin, 1950), p. 23.

serious reduction in our own defense the War Cabinet and the Chiefs of Staff felt no anxiety."[6] Recurring to the situation in the spring of 1941, he observes: "I did not regard invasion as a serious danger in April, 1941, since proper preparations had been made against it."[7] . . .

A powerful voice from across the Atlantic joined the chorus of those who insisted that the lend-lease bill would keep America out of war. Winston Churchill, whose private letters to Roosevelt had long been filled with pleas for American warlike action, broadcast this reassurance to the American people on February 9, 1941:

We do not need the gallant armies which are forming throughout the American Union. We do not need them this year, nor next year, nor any year I can foresee. But we need urgently an immense and continuing supply of war materials. . . . We shall not fail or falter, we shall not weaken or tire. . . . *Give us the tools and we will do the job.* [Italics supplied.]

Viewing this broadcast in retrospect, Churchill frankly observes: "This could only be an interim pronouncement. Far more was needed. But we did our best."[8]

On any sober, realistic appraisal of British and Axis strength this was assurance which could not be fulfilled. But it was what many Americans wished to hear. Lend-lease was carried because the minority of all-out interventionists were reinforced by a larger number who hoped, and were given every assurance to this effect by Administration spokesmen, that unlimited subsidies of munitions and supplies would buy America out of active participation in the war.

There were voices of opposition. Senator Taft saw as "the important thing about this bill" that "its provisions in effect give the President power to carry on an undeclared war all over the world, in which America would do everything except actually put soldiers in the front-line trenches where the fighting is." The Senator could not see (and events would soon bear him out) how we could long conduct such a war without being in "the shooting as well as the service-of-supply end." Senator C. Wayland Brooks, of Illinois, called it a "war bill with war powers, with the deliberate intention of becoming involved in other peoples' wars." Colonel Lindbergh described lend-lease as "a major step to getting us into war." The veteran Socialist leader, Norman Thomas, foresaw as consequences of the lend-lease legislation "total war on two oceans and five continents; a war likely to result in stalemate, perhaps in such a break-up of western civilization that Stalin, with his vast armies and loyal communist followers, will be the victor."

The bill became law on March 11, 1941. The vote was 265 to 165 in the House, 60 to 31 in the Senate. These were substantial, but not overwhelming majorities. Had the measure been frankly presented as a measure of limited war, which it was, it is most improbable that it could have been passed.

While Congress was discussing lend-lease, important American and British staff talks were taking place in Washington in an atmosphere of extreme secrecy. At the very time when anxious Congressmen were being assured that the lend-lease bill was designed to avoid war, these military and naval experts were adopting a report which took American participation in the war for granted. The principal conclusions of this report were phrased as follows:

The staff conference assumes that *when* the United States becomes involved in war with Germany it will at the same time engage in

[6] *Ibid.*, pp. 4–5.
[7] *Ibid.*, p. 238.
[8] *Ibid.*, p. 128.

war with Italy. In these circumstances the possibility of a state of war arising between Japan and an association of the United States, the British Commonwealth and its allies, including the Netherlands East Indies, must be taken into account.

Since Germany is the predominant member of the Axis powers, the Atlantic and European area is considered the decisive theatre. The principal United States effort will be exerted in that theatre, and operations in other theatres will be conducted in such a manner as to facilitate that effort.[9] [Italics supplied.]

The use of the word *when*, not *if*, was certainly suggestive of the Administration's attitude.

Typical of the furtive methods by which Roosevelt edged the country into a state of undeclared war was the noteworthy care taken to conceal these American-British talks (not only their content, but the fact that they were taking place) from the knowledge of Congress. This is made clear by Robert E. Sherwood when he writes:

Although the common-law alliance involved the United States in no undercover commitments, and no violation of the Constitution, the very existence of any American-British joint plans, however tentative, had to be kept utterly secret. It is an ironic fact that in all probability no great damage would have been done had the details of these plans fallen into the hands of the Germans and the Japanese; whereas, had they fallen into the hands of Congress and the press, American preparation for war might have been well nigh wrecked and ruined.[10]

There could scarcely be a more candid admission, from a source favorable to Roosevelt, that America was stealthily maneuvered into war behind the backs and without the knowledge of the elected representatives of the American people. A study of the Congressional debates and private talks with some members of that body confirm this view. Even members of the Senate and House Foreign Relations Committees were kept very much in the dark as to what the President was doing or intending to do. As Nathaniel Peffer subsequently wrote in an issue of *Harper's Magazine:*

When, for example, the United States traded to Great Britain destroyers for bases, it was for all practical purposes entering the war. Congress had no voice in that. It was notified later by the President, but then the fact was accomplished. Similarly, when the President ordered the freezing of Japanese assets in this country in July, 1941, he was decreeing a state of war with Japan. And with respect to that act the Senate Committee on Foreign Relations had no more to say than a similar number of North Dakota wheat farmers.[11]

Like the Roman god Janus, Roosevelt in the prewar period had two faces. For the American people, for the public record, there was the face of bland assurance that his first concern was to keep the country out of war. But in more intimate surroundings the Chief Executive often assumed that America was already involved in war. . . .

The next milestone on the road to war in the Atlantic was the decision to employ American naval forces to insure the deliveries of munitions and supplies to Britain. There had been much discussion of naval convoys during the debate on the Lend-Lease Act. Roosevelt stated on January 21 that he had no intention of using his powers under this bill to convoy merchant ships. "Convoys," he said,

[9] See JCC (Joint Congressional Committee on the Investigation of the Pearl Harbor Attack) Part 15, Ex. 49, 50, 51.
[10] *Roosevelt and Hopkins*, pp. 273–74.

[11] Nathaniel Peffer, "The Split in Our Foreign Policy," *Harper's Magazine,* 187 (August, 1943), p. 198.

"mean shooting and shooting means war."

The Lend-Lease Act as finally passed contained several amendments clearly designed to prevent the President from using it as an authorization for carrying on undeclared war. According to these amendments, nothing in the Act was to authorize convoying by United States naval vessels, the entry of any American vessel into a combat area or the change of existing law relating to the use of the land and naval forces of the United States, "except insofar as such use relates to the manufacture, procurement and repair of defense articles, the communication of information and other noncombatant purposes enumerated in this act."

As soon as the Lend-Lease Act became law Roosevelt characteristically set out to find a means of convoying supplies which could be plausibly called by some other name. "Patrol" seemed to fill the needs of the situation.

The bellicose Secretaries of War and the Navy, Stimson and Knox, had agreed toward the end of March "that the crisis is coming very soon and that convoying is the only solution and that it must come practically at once.[12] However, the plan which Roosevelt finally approved on April 24 was less bold than the open dispatch of convoys, although it achieved much the same purpose. Under this scheme the American Navy was assigned the responsibility of patrolling the Atlantic west of a median point represented by 25° longitude. Within this area United States warships and naval planes would search out German raiders and submarines and broadcast their position to the British Navy. Roosevelt and Hopkins drafted a cable to Churchill, outlining this scheme and suggesting that the British keep their convoys west of the new line up to the northwestern approaches.[13]

With typical indirection Roosevelt even in private Cabinet meetings tried to represent this as merely a defensive move, designed to protect the Western Hemisphere against attack. The more candid Stimson recorded in his diary for April 24:

He [Roosevelt] kept reverting to the fact that the forces in the Atlantic were merely going to be a patrol to watch for any aggression and report that to America. I answered there, with a smile on my face, saying: "But you are not going to report the presence of the German Fleet to the Americas. You are going to report it to the British Fleet." I wanted him to be honest with himself. To me it seems a clearly hostile act to the Germans, and I am prepared to take the responsibility of it. He seems to be trying to hide it into the character of a purely reconnaisance action, which it clearly is not.[14]

Even before the patrol system had been adopted, the American Navy had been stepping far beyond the bounds of hemisphere defense. The Congressional Pearl Harbor investigation turned up two interesting letters from Admiral Harold Stark, Chief of Naval Operations, to Admiral Husband E. Kimmel, commander in chief of the Pacific fleet. In the first of these, dated April 4, 1941, Stark wrote: "The question as to our entry into the war seems to be *when,* and not *whether.*" The second is more specific about military preparations on the other side of the Atlantic:

I am enclosing a memo on convoy which I drew up primarily to give the President a picture of what is now being done, what we would propose to do if we convoyed, and of our ability to do it. . . .

Our officers who have been studying the positions for bases in the British Isles have returned, and we have decided on immedi-

---

[12] Henry L. Stimson and McGeorge Bundy, *On Active Service,* p. 367.

[13] Sherwood, *op. cit.,* pp. 291–92.
[14] Stimson and Bundy, *op. cit.,* pp. 368–69.

ate construction of 1 destroyer base and 1 seaplane base in Northern Ireland. We are also studying Scotland-Iceland bases for further support of the protective force for shipping in the northward approaches to Britain.

All this did not harmonize with the President's pre-election promises that "this country is not going to war." But with no election in prospect that was no brake on the gradual slide toward open belligerence.

Roosevelt in a press conference on May 16 referred to a subject which evidently appealed to his imagination, since he raised it on several other occasions. This was the presidential right to wage undeclared war, as illustrated by such precedents as the clash with France during the Administration of John Adams and with the Barbary pirates when Jefferson was President. Roosevelt declared that the Germans were really pirates. On the same day Knox announced: "It is impossible to exaggerate the mortal danger of our country at this moment."

Stimson had already sounded a call to war in a radio address of May 6, which ended as follows:

Today a small group of evil leaders have taught the young men of Germany that the freedom of other men and nations must be destroyed. Today those young men are ready to die for that perverted conviction. Unless we on our side are ready to sacrifice and, if need be, die for the conviction that the freedom of America must be saved, it will not be saved. Only by a readiness for the same sacrifice can that freedom be preserved.

Roosevelt himself on May 27, 1941, delivered a speech which seemed designed to scare the American people into approving warlike measures. "The war," the President said, "is approaching the brink of the Western Hemisphere itself. It is coming very close to home." He spoke of "the Nazi book of world conquest" and declared the Nazis planned to treat the Latin American countries as they were now treating the Balkans. Then, according to the President, the United States and Canada would be strangled. American labor would have to compete with slave labor and the American farmer would get for his products exactly what Hitler wanted to give. Roosevelt outlined a very elastic and expansive conception of defense requirements.

"The attack on the United States can begin with the domination of any base which menaces our security—north or south."

Therefore:

Old-fashioned common sense calls for the use of strategy that will prevent such an enemy from gaining a foothold in the first place.

We have, accordingly, extended our patrol in North and South Atlantic waters. We are steadily adding more and more ships and planes to that patrol. It is well known that the strength of the Atlantic Fleet has been greatly increased during the last year, and that it is constantly being built up. . . .[15] We are thus being forewarned. We shall be on our guard against efforts to establish Nazi bases closer to our hemisphere.

The speech ended in a bellicose climax:

We in the Americas will decide for ourselves whether, and when, and where, our American interests are attacked or our security is threatened.

We are placing our armed forces in strategic military position.

We will not hesitate to use our armed forces to repel attack.

There was also a declaration of a state of "unlimited national emergency." However, there was a sense of anticlimax

---

[15] This fact was doubtless "well known" to the Japanese Intelligence Service and was one consideration which prompted the attack on Pearl Harbor.

when Roosevelt in his press conference on the following day denied any intention to institute convoys or to press for the repeal of the Neutrality Act.

In the retrospect of years, how well founded was the sense of national mortal peril which the President, the more bellicose members of his Cabinet, and a host of individuals and organizations tried to cultivate in the American people? In the light of the ascertainable facts, which are now pretty well known, one cannot but feel that the picture was grossly exaggerated.

What was the over-all military picture in May 1941? There was no longer serious danger of a Nazi invasion of England.[16] The American and British surface fleets were enormously stronger than the combined Axis naval strength. There was, therefore, not the slightest prospect that German armies could cross the Atlantic in force.

At that time there were constant rumors of German infiltration into French North Africa. A favorite scare story was that Hitler's legions would move ino Dakar (itself a long jump from North Africa) and then move across the Atlantic into Brazil. Commentators who spread these stories never took the trouble to explain how it would be possible to transport substantial forces across the ocean in the face of superior American and British naval power.

And we know now that there was never any factual basis for these rumors. The reports of two American representatives on the spot, Robert D. Murphy, in North Africa, and Consul Thomas C. Wasson, in Dakar, are in agreement on this point; Murphy's reports show that there were about two hundred Germans, mostly connected with the armistice commission, in

North Africa. Wasson informed the State Department that the only Germans in Dakar were a few Jewish refugees.[17]

The fall of Germany and the capture of the Nazi archives revealed no evidence of any plan for the invasion of North or South America. It is reasonable to assume that a victorious Nazi Germany would have been an uncomfortable neighbor, just as a victorious Soviet Russia is today. But there is no proof that Hitler envisaged the American continent as part of his empire.

And there is a strong element of overheated fantasy in the vision of American labor ground down by the competition of slave labor, of the American farmer condemned to take what Hitler would give. The Nazis could scarcely have made slave labor more prevalent than it is in Stalin's huge postwar empire. American labor standards have not been depressed as a result. And the level of American farm prices depends far more on the state of supply and on the willingness of American taxpayers to pay subsidies than it does on the character of foreign political regimes.

Unquestionably the war was not going well for Britain in the spring of 1941. The Germans had overrun the Balkans and had seized Crete by an air-borne operation. The reconquest of Europe from Hitler and the crushing of the Nazi regime in its own territory, the obvious war aim of Churchill and Roosevelt, gave every prospect of being a difficult, long, and costly enterprise.

But the suggestion that the Western Hemisphere was in imminent peril can fairly be dismissed as a fraudulent exaggeration. The fraud and the exaggeration are all the greater if one considers that both the American and the British governments were in possession of reli-

[16] This point is recognized by Churchill several times in *The Grand Alliance*.

[17] William L. Langer, *Our Vichy Gamble*, p. 87.

able information to the effect that Hitler's main military strength would soon be hurled against Russia. The most fevered alarmist imagination could scarcely envisage Hitler's simultaneously invading Russia and mounting an offensive against the American continent.

Not all Americans were convinced by the dire forebodings of Roosevelt's "unlimited national emergency" speech. Senator Taft commented drily in a nationwide broadcast:

The whole argument of the war party that Hitler can conquer the United States or dominate the seas that surround us has just about faded into the discard. But the President now lays more stress on the danger to our trade. He threatens the American workman that his wages and hours would be fixed by Hitler. . . . What is Japan to do with its silk except sell it to us? We take over half Brazil's coffee. Even if the Nazis dominated the Netherlands East Indies there would be nothing to do with the rubber except sell it to us. It is utterly ridiculous to suppose that our trade with South America or Asia or even Europe will be wiped out.

✻   ✻   ✻

In view of the agreements about a joint warning to Japan and about military action on the foreign soil of the East Atlantic islands, Roosevelt was not candid when he declared after [his "Atlantic Charter" conference with Churchill] that there were no new commitments and that the country was no closer to war. To be sure, something had occurred on the last day of the conference which was calculated to impose a brake on a too-headlong interventionist course. The renewal of the Selective Service Act, enacted in 1940 for one year, squeezed through the House of Representatives by only one vote. . . .

Roosevelt's next move toward war in the Atlantic was the proclamation, without consulting Congress or obtaining congressional sanction, of a "shoot at sight" campaign against Axis submarines. The pretext was an exchange of shots between the *Greer,* an American destroyer bound for Iceland, and a German submarine on September 5. Roosevelt misrepresented this incident as a wanton, unprovoked attack on the American vessel. . . .

The announcement of the Presidential shooting war in the Atlantic was followed by more serious clashes. The destroyer *Kearny* was hit by a torpedo with the loss of eleven lives on October 17 and on October 30 the *Reuben James,* another destroyer, was sunk with a casualty list of 155 members of her crew.

Roosevelt struck a new high bellicose note in his Navy Day speech of October 27:

The shooting has started. And history has recorded who fired the first shot. In the long run, however, all that will matter is who fired the last shot. . . .

I say that we do not propose to take this lying down.

Today, in the face of this newest and greatest challenge of them all, we Americans have cleared our decks and taken our battle stations. We stand ready in the defense of our nation and the faith of our fathers to do what God has given us the power to see as our full duty.

But the majority of the American people remained markedly indifferent to these warlike appeals. The contrast between the President's categorical pledges not to get into war in 1940 (when the danger to Britain was certainly far greater than it was after Hitler attacked Russia) and his present obvious efforts to get into hostilities at any price was too strong.

Some public-opinion polls taken during this period are not very revealing. Much depended on who was conducting them, on how questions were phrased, on which groups in the community were reached. But Congress was a pretty reliable barometer of the mood of the nation. The one-vote majority by which selective service was renewed was one signal of the aversion to the idea of a second crusade. Another unmistakable signal was given only three weeks before Pearl Harbor.

The President had asked for authority to arm American merchant ships and to send these ships into war zones. This amounted to a repeal of the Neutrality Act, which Roosevelt had done everything in his power to circumvent. This proposal was still far short of a declaration of war. But it proved extremely difficult to get legislation providing for these changes through Congress. The bill passed the Senate, 50–37, on November 7 and narrowly escaped defeat in the House, where the vote was 212–194, a week later. A change of ten votes would have given the Administration a severe setback. Very strong pressure from the White House was put on the representatives, including promises of judgeships and other federal appointments where these would do the most good.

Interventionists at this time freely admitted and deplored the reluctance of the American people to plunge into the slaughter. The Committee to Defend America by Aiding the Allies took a full-page advertisement to lament the "dreadfully narrow margin" by which the bill authorizing the arming of merchant ships had passed. Walter Lippmann wrote in September 1941 of "the low state of our war morale." Stanley High, another publicist who favored intervention, commented regretfully on Lippmann's observation in a letter published in the *New York Herald Tribune:*

"No, the whole truth about our war morale is not that it is now in a slump. Measured by what we are up against, it was never in anything else."

An investigation of the alleged attempt of the moving-picture industry to promote a war psychosis was started in the Senate in September. John T. Flynn, one of the active leaders of the America First Committee, accused film producers of "using propaganda to raise the war hysteria in this country, to inflame the people of the United States to a state of mind where they will be willing to go to war with Germany." He cited *Underground* as one of some fifty films designed to arouse feelings of hatred and vengeance.

The radio and the press, like the films, were overwhelmingly on the interventionist side by the autumn of 1941. Flynn asserted that in three days he had counted 127 interventionist broadcasts, compared with six on the other side.

And yet, with all the sparks that were being generated, the people failed to catch fire. Hundreds of chapters of the America First Committee pledged themselves to work for the defeat of congressmen who had voted to repeal the Neutrality Act. Francis P. Miller, an extreme interventionist, was defeated by a Republican in an off-year election in Fairfax County, Virginia, in November 1941. This was a district in which a Democratic victory was normally taken for granted.

The autumn of 1941 was a difficult period for Roosevelt. He was under pressure from those members of his Cabinet, Stimson and Knox and Morgenthau, who favored stronger action. He was exposed to a barrage of transatlantic pleas from Churchill. He had stretched his Presidential powers to the limit. He had provoked shooting incidents in the Atlantic and misrepresented these incidents when they occurred. But he had not aroused much will to war in the country.

General Wood, chairman of the America First Committee, challenged Roosevelt to put the issue of a declaration of war to the test of a vote in Congress. This was a challenge which the President could not accept, in view of the close vote on the less provocative question of repealing the Neutrality Act. Robert E. Sherwood tells how gloomy the situation seemed at this time to those who wished to get America into the war:

The truth was that, as the world situation became more desperately critical, and as the limitless peril came closer and closer to the United States, isolationist sentiment became ever more strident in expression and aggressive in action, and Roosevelt was relatively powerless to combat it. He had said everything "short of war" that could be said. He had no more tricks left. The hat from which he had pulled so many rabbits was empty.[18]

But just when the situation in the Atlantic seemed very unpromising, from the standpoint of speedy full involvement in war, rescue for the Administration came from the Pacific. The Japanese attack on Pearl Harbor, followed by Hitler's declaration of war, extricated Roosevelt from one of the most difficult dilemmas in which a statesman can find himself— the dilemma of having led his people halfway into war.

The eleven principal steps by which Roosevelt took America into undeclared war in the Atlantic may be briefly summarized as follows:

(1) The repeal of the arms embargo in November 1939.

[18] Sherwood, *op. cit.*, pp. 382–83.

(2) The trade of destroyers for bases in September 1940.

(3) Enactment of the Lend-Lease Act in March 1941.

(4) The secret American-British staff talks, January-March 1941.

(5) The institution of "patrols" in the North Atlantic on April 24.

(6) The sending of American laborers to build a naval base in Northern Ireland.

(7) The blocking of German credits in the United States and the closing of consulates in the early summer of 1941.

(8) The occupation of Iceland by American troops on July 7.

(9) The Atlantic Conference, August 9–12.

(10) The shoot-at-sight orders given to American warships and announced on September 11.

(11) Authorization for the arming of merchant ships and the sending of merchant ships into war zones in November 1941.

The first three of these steps were accompanied by loud protestations that they were designed to keep America at peace, not to get it into war. Several of the other measures were taken without consulting Congress in an atmosphere of exaggerated alarmism, secrecy, contrived confusion and official misrepresentation of facts. The entire record may be usefully set against Roosevelt's repeated categorical assurances that his principal aim was to keep America out of war. Seldom if ever in American history was there such a gulf between appearances and realities, between Presidential words and Presidential deeds.

Charles Callan Tansill: BACK DOOR TO WAR

A major issue emerging from the controversy over Pearl Harbor concerns the conflicting judgments on the nature of the war. In the selection below, Charles C. Tansill builds a case to show that the United States misunderstood the problem facing the Japanese. Along with other students of American foreign policy like A. Whitney Griswold and George F. Kennan, Tansill believes that Japan foresaw the probability that Russian influence would become dominant over a decadent China if Japan withdrew. He charges Stimson with perpetuation of the myth that American interests were more closely identified with China than Japan. In addition to the work from which this selection is taken, Professor Tansill of Georgetown University is the author of an outstanding revisionist history of the cause of our entry into World War I, America Goes to War (1938) as well as a number of other books and articles in diplomatic history.

CONTINUED FRICTION WITH JAPAN POINTS TOWARDS INEVITABLE WAR

Congress Enacts an Exclusion Law Which Angers Japan

As American statesmen looked from the troubled scenes in China to the quiet landscapes in Japan, it was not with relief but with suspicion that they viewed the placid picture of Old Nippon. The orderly ways of empire grated upon the sensibilities of many Americans who preferred the uneasy atmosphere of democracy to the regulated rhythm of the Mikado's Government. Since 1913, Japan had been under almost constant attack by the Department of State. The Wilson Administration had led a sustained assault against Japan along several fronts, and the inauguration of a Republican Administration in 1921 had led to the calling of the Washington Conference for the express purpose of checking Japanese plans for expansion. The climate of opinion in the United States was definitely hostile to Japan, and it was inevitable that clouds of misunderstanding between the two countries should gather along the diplomatic horizon. The first threat of a storm came in connection with the immigration question.

After the close of the World War there was an increasing fear in the United States that the war-impoverished countries of Europe would send a huge wave of immigration to American shores. On May 19, 1921, in order to prevent such a contingency, Congress enacted a law that limited the number of aliens of any particular nationality that would be granted admission to the United States in any one year to 3 per cent of the "number of foreign-born persons of such nationality resident in the United States" in the year 1910. Some months later a new act was framed which reduced the annual admission of any nationality to 2 per cent of the foreign-born population of that nationality resident in the United States in 1890.[1] A high dyke had been erected against the expected wave of immigration.

It was soon apparent that this new legislation would not be used merely to supplement the gentlemen's agreement with Japan which since 1907 had controlled the immigration of laborers from that country. In 1921 a movement began in the Far West to exclude by legislation any further immigration of Japanese laborers.

Background of the Manchurian Incident

JAPAN IS WORRIED OVER THE SPREAD OF COMMUNISM IN CHINA. The outcome of the conflict between China and Soviet Russia in 1929 had important implications for Japan. First of all, it was clear that Russia had violated the provisions of the Sino-Russian agreement of 1924 which prohibited the spread of communistic propaganda in China. The vast amount of data seized by Chinese police in the Harbin Consulate left no doubt on this point. Russian denials carried no conviction to Japanese minds, and the fact that Chang Hsueh-liang had to fight alone against Soviet armed forces indicated that Chiang Kai-shek was either too weak to guard the frontiers of Manchuria effectively or was not deeply disturbed by the Russian chastisement of the war lord of the Three Eastern Provinces. The Japanese bastions of defense in North China were in evident danger.

This fact seemed apparent to Japanese statesmen when they looked at the ominous failure of Chiang Kai-shek to cope with communist armies. In December 1930, Chiang mobilized troops, from Hunan, Hopeh, and Kiangsi provinces and sent them against the Communists. The Reds soon annihilated the Eighteenth Corps under General Chang Hueitsan and caused the rapid retreat of the Fiftieth Corps. In February 1931, General Ho Ying-chin was given three army corps to attack the Reds but by May his forces were compelled to withdraw. In July, Chiang Kai-shek himself led a large army to the Nanchang front, but accomplished nothing decisive.[2] The Red menace was daily becoming more formidable and Japanese fears rapidly increased. The only way to insure Japanese security was through adequate measures of defense in Manchuria. These might violate some shadowy rights of sovereignty that China had over Manchuria, but these rights had not been successfully asserted since 1912 and would soon be extinguished by Russia if Japan took no action. For Japan, expansion in Manchuria was a national imperative. . . .

To Japan it appeared obvious that Manchuria was essential to her as a bastion of defense and as the keystone of her economic structure. Her statesmen hoped that the Department of State would recognize that North China was just as important to Japan as the Caribbean area was to the United States. The American Government had sent military forces to Haiti and to the Dominican Republic for the purpose of establishing administrations that would be responsive to American desires.[3] This armed inter-

[1] A. Whitney Griswold, *The Far Eastern Policy of the United States* (New York, 1938), pp. 369–70.

[2] *Communism in China, Document A, Appendix No. 3* (Tokyo, 1932), pp. 3–5. This document was published by the Japanese Government as a part of the case of Japan. For a sympathetic account of the struggle of Chiang Kai-shek with the Chinese Communists see T'ang Leang-Li, *Suppressing Communist Banditry in China* (Shanghai, 1934), chap. 5.

[3] Hallett Abend, *New York Times*, November 4, 1931.

vention had been so recent and so effective that it led the American chargé in Peking to send a dispatch to Secretary Kellogg which ended on a significant note: "We cannot oppose Japanese plans in Manchuria ethically in view of measures we have taken in our correspondingly vital zone—the Caribbean. . . ."[4]

Japan was well aware of the danger that this Red tide might roll over most of China. In the documents presented to the Lytton Commission in 1932, emphasis was placed upon this communist menace and upon the apparent inability of the Chinese Nationalist Government to control it.[5] It seemed to Tokyo that Japanese interests in North China were about to be crushed between the millstones of Chinese nationalism and Russian bolshevism. An appeal to the League of Nations would accomplish little. Chinese nationalism had found a sympathetic audience in the Western powers. Most of them were inclined to accept the fictions and pretensions put forward by the Nanking Government. The Japanese position in North China was in grave danger of being infiltrated by Reds or successfully attacked by fervent Chinese Nationalists whose patriotism had turned into a "flame of hatred."[6]

The dilemma that faced Japan is clearly and cogently stated by George Sokolsky who was used as an intermediary between China and Japan in 1931:

It needs to be recalled here that in 1931 the last efforts were made to reconcile these countries [China and Japan]. Actually, I was an instrument in that attempted reconciliation, going to Japan from China to hold meetings with Baron Shidehara, Minister of

Foreign Affairs, and others. I can say that the Japanese attitude was conciliatory; the Chinese, on the whole, antagonistic. . . . Two forces were at work to keep China and Japan quarreling: Soviet Russia and the League of Nations. Soviet Russia had been engaged since 1924 in an active program of stirring hate among the Chinese people against all foreigners except the Russians, but particularly against the British and the Japanese. The League of Nations secretariat was developing in China a field of widespread activity through its agent, Dr. Ludwic Rajchmann, who was spending most of his time in China. Rajchmann was violently anti-Japanese, although Japan was a member of the League of Nations and Rajchmann an employee. Rajchmann is a Pole and is now associated with the United Nations.[7]

Secretary Stimson Prepares a Path to War

One of the reasons why Japan was "conciliatory" towards China in 1931 was because of the shaky structure of Japanese finance. A war with China might lead to very serious consequences. On September 18, 1931, the American press published a summary of a report made by Dr. Harold G. Moulton, of the Brookings Institution, on economic conditions in the Japanese Empire. This survey had been undertaken upon the invitation of the Japanese Minister of Finance. In conclusion the summary stated that "military retrenchment, continuation of peaceful relations with the United States, and sharp restriction of the present rates of population are all essential if serious economic and financial difficulties in Japan are to be averted. . . . A balanced budget and tax reduction can be accomplished only if military outlays are curtailed."[8]

It was only with the greatest reluctance, therefore, that Japanese states-

[4] Ferdinand L. Mayer to Secretary Kellogg, Peking, November 22, 1927. 894.51 So 8/4 MS, Department of State.
[5] Communism in China, Document A, Appendix No. 3 (Tokyo, 1932).
[6] Lytton Report, op. cit., p. 19.

[7] George Sokolsky, "These Days," Washington Times-Herald, March 14, 1951.
[8] Ware, op. cit., p. 206.

men consented to support a program of expansion in Manchuria. After it was apparent that the Japanese Kwantung Army had seized certain cities in North China, Hugh Byas, writing from Tokyo, reported that the sudden movement of troops had not been "foreseen by the Japanese Government and had not been preventable.[9] Byas, as well as many other veteran observers in the Far East, had great confidence in the pacific disposition of Baron Shidehara, the Japanese Minister of Foreign Relations. Secretary Stimson shared this view and at first he was anxious to refrain from exerting too much pressure upon the Japanese Government because he feared such a policy would play into the hands of the militarists. . . .

The bombing of Chinchow by Japanese planes on October 8 provoked Stimson to take more vigorous action to preserve peace. He now began to consider the employment of sanctions against Japan in order to compel her to "respect the great peace treaties."[10] On October 10 he secured the President's approval of a suggestion to have an American representative participate in all the sessions of the League Council which dealt with the enforcement of the Kellogg-Briand Pact. . . .

On October 17, with Mr. Gilbert in attendance, the Council of the League decided upon a joint invocation of the Kellogg-Briand Pact. After Stimson had been assured that the League would take action he sent (October 20) identic notes to China and Japan reminding them of their obligations under the pact.[11] The Council took the further step (October 24) of calling upon Japan to "begin immediately with the withdrawal of its troops into the railway zone" of the South Manchuria Railway. This withdrawal should be completed by November 16.[12]

Edwin Neville, the American chargé at Tokyo, regarded this directive of the League as inopportune and ineffective and he requested the Department of State to refrain from giving it any support. American co-operation in this particular case would "weaken American influence in Japan" and would not "accomplish anything" in settling the Manchurian dispute.[13]

Stimson paid scant attention to this advice. On November 5, Ambassador Forbes handed to the Japanese Foreign Minister a memorandum which closely followed the phraseology of the League resolution with the exception that no time limit was set for the withdrawal of the Japanese troops.[14] On November 19 he fired another shot in this barrage against Japan. In a conversation with Debuchi he warned him that the American Government might publish the diplomatic correspondence that had passed between the Foreign Office and the Department of State and thus mobilize world opinion against the actions of Japanese militarists.[15]

After this thrust against Japan, Stimson once more turned to the League and explained the basis of American action.

[9] *New York Times*, September 19, 1931.
[10] Henry L. Stimson, *The Far Eastern Crisis: Recollections and Observations* (New York, 1936), pp. 51–57.
[11] Secretary Stimson to the American Minister in China and to the American chargé d'affaires in Japan, October 20, 1931. *Ibid.*, p. 275.

[12] *Foreign Relations: Japan, 1931–1941*, I, 29–30.
[13] Chargé in Japan (Neville) to Secretary Stimson, Tokyo, November 4, 1931. *Foreign Relations, 1931*, III, 366–67.
[14] Memorandum of a conversation between Ambassador Forbes (Tokyo) with the Japanese Minister for Foreign Affairs (Shidehara), November 5, 1931. *Ibid.*, pp. 375–80.
[15] Memorandum by the Secretary of State of a conversation with the Japanese Ambassador (Debuchi), November 19, 1931. *Foreign Relations: Japan, 1931–1941*, I, 44–46.

Pressure from President Hoover had softened the tone of his notes. When Stimson in Cabinet meetings began to talk about coercing Japan by all "means short of actual use of armed force," the President informed him that "this was simply the road to war itself and he would have none of it."[16]

Stimson, therefore, instructed Ambassador Dawes to tell certain members of the League Council that, while the American fleet would not take any adverse action against any embargo that would be enforced against Japanese commerce, it should be clearly understood that the United States would not participate in any economic sanctions. America would assist in mobilizing public opinion against Japan and would refuse to recognize "any treaties that were created under military force."[17]

Under the impact of this American pressure, Shidehara desperately strove to modify the policy of the militarists in Tokyo and on November 27 he was able to put a brief stop to the Manchurian advance. But the Japanese Cabinet fell two weeks later and these futile peace gestures ceased. On January 2, 1932, Chinchow was captured and the Japanese conquestion of Manchuria was complete.

Before this took place Elihu Root, thoroughly alarmed by the active measures Secretary Stimson was taking to stop Japanese expansion in Manchuria, wrote the Secretary a long letter of protest. Root had been Secretary of State from 1905 to 1909 and had negotiated the Root-Takahira Agreement that had given Japan a green light in Manchuria.

He now warned Stimson about "getting entangled in League measures which we have no right to engage in against Japan." He also alluded to Japan's special interests in Manchuria through a long period of years, and spoke of the need for Japan to protect herself in a political sense against "the dagger aimed at her heart."

Root was a realist who did not want war with Japan. Stimson was a pacifist who loved peace so much he was always ready to fight for it. He wholeheartedly subscribed to the slogan—perpetual war for perpetual peace. In his answer to Root he expressed the belief that his intervention in the Manchurian muddle was necessary to save the whole structure of the peace treaties. He was the Atlas on whose stooping shoulders world peace was precariously balanced. A "new advance by Japan" would "undoubtedly create much adverse and even hostile sentiment in this country and much pressure upon us for some kind of action." As a man of action he was not inclined to draw back into any shell of neutrality. . . .[18]

For the next two months Stimson had to stand responsible for the nonrecognition policy without any help from Great Britain, but there were certain factors that slowly pushed the Foreign Office into line with the Department of State. Britain had extensive business interests in Shanghai, and when the Japanese, on January 28, 1932, opened an offensive against the Chinese Nineteenth Route Army stationed in that city, the situation took on a new aspect.

. . . Time and British big business were working on his side. On February 16 the League Council sent an appeal to Japan for the purpose of dissuading her from making a full-scale attack upon

[16] Ray L. Wilbur and Arthur M. Hyde, *The Hoover Policies* (New York, 1937), p. 603.
[17] Memorandum of a trans-Atlantic telephone conversation between Secretary Stimson and Ambassador Dawes, November 19, 1931. *Foreign Relations, 1931,* III, 488–98.

[18] Secretary Stimson to Elihu Root, December 14, 1931, Strictly Personal and Confidential, Box 129, Root Papers, Library of Congress.

Shanghai. In this appeal Japan was pointed out as the responsible party in the Far Eastern conflict, and she was reminded of her obligations under the Covenant of the League of Nations and under the provisions of the Nine-Power Treaty.[19] On March 11 the Assembly of the League took a bolder step when it adopted a resolution which declared that it was "incumbent upon the members of the League of Nations not to recognize any situation, treaty or agreement which may be brought about by means contrary to the Covenant of the League of Nations or to the Pact of Paris."[20]

Secretary Stimson had at last maneuvered the League of Nations into a formal approval of the nonrecognition theory. It was a fateful step along a "dead-end" street of fear and frustration, and its inevitable consequence was America's involvement in World War II.[21]

SECRETARY STIMSON PRODUCES A PATTERN OF WAR

As one means of coping with the Japanese advance in North China, Stimson sent Joseph C. Grew to Tokyo as the American Ambassador. When Grew arrived in Japan in June 1932, the press was friendly and the Emperor was as agreeable as Mr. Grew's deafness permitted him to be. But the shadows of the Manchurian adventure fell across the threshold of the American Embassy and Grew soon realized that they would probably deepen and lengthen despite all his efforts to banish them with the bright light of some new Japanese-American understanding.

The main barrier across the road to friendly relations was the Stimson doctrine itself. The Japanese Government was determined to recognize Manchukuo in defiance of adverse opinion in the United States and in Europe. Secure control over North China appeared to Japanese statesmen, regardless of party affiliations, as a national necessity. As a source of essential raw materials and as a market for manufactured goods, Manchuria had special importance for Japan. Presidents Theodore Roosevelt and Woodrow Wilson had been willing to regard certain portions of North China as a Japanese sphere of influence, and the language of the Root-Takahira and the Lansing-Ishii agreements was so vaguely fertile that Japanese aspirations had enjoyed a rapid growth. Theodore

[19] Irving S. Friedman, *British Relations with China, 1931–1939* (New York, 1940), p. 33.

[20] The consul at Geneva (Gilbert) to Secretary Stimson, Geneva, March 15, 1932. *Foreign Relations, 1932*, III, 585–86. Westel W. Willoughby, *The Sino-Japanese Controversy and the League of Nations* (Baltimore, 1935), pp. 299–301.

[21] The dangers that were inherent in the Far Eastern situation were discussed at length by the British Prime Minister (Ramsay MacDonald) in a conversation with Mr. Atherton, the American chargé d'affaires at London, on April 4, 1932: "In substance the Prime Minister said that it was foreseen some time ago by critics of the League that members might well be actually in a state of war without a formal declaration of war, in order to escape the penalties placed upon war by the Covenant. This was in fact what had happened in the present instance, although the Chinese had almost 'put the fat in the fire.' During the last Far Eastern discussions in Geneva the Chinese had drawn up a resolution which a League representative agreed formally to present. This resolution declared that Japan by her actions was in fact in a state of war with members of the League.

"The League representative showed this resolution to Sir John Simon who said that he would have nothing to do with it and that if it were presented he would deny all knowledge of it. Eventually the resolution just escaped presentation, but the Prime Minister said that this showed how near Japan had been to open conflict with members of the League." 793.94/4965. *Confidential file*, MS, Department of State.

Roosevelt, after boldly plucking the Panama pear, could not turn a deaf ear to Japanese pleas for a bite of Manchurian melon. And Woodrow Wilson, deep in his preparations for a crusade against wicked Germany, could not look too closely into Japanese motives in Manchuria. Encouraged by these friendly gestures of American Presidents, Japanese armies moved into many parts of North China. When Stimson suddenly flashed a red light of warning against any further advance, the Japanese Government made no real effort to obey the signal. Their Manchurian machine had gained too much momentum to be stopped by an American traffic cop who merely blew a tin whistle of nonrecognition.

The efforts of European statesmen were just as futile as those of Secretary Stimson. The Lytton Commission, appointed under the terms of the League resolution of December 10, 1931, reached Tokyo on February 29, 1932, for a series of conferences with Japanese statesmen and with representatives of various Japanese organizations. From April 20 to June 4 the commission took testimony in Manchuria, and then returned to Tokyo for a brief sojourn. It finally moved to Peiping to complete the task of drafting a formal report.

While the commission was in Tokyo, Major General Frank R. McCoy talked freely to Ambassador Grew. He assured the ambassador that the commission was of the opinion that Japan's action in Manchuria was based on two false premises: the argument of self-defense and the argument of self-determination. The commission was also convinced that the erection of a puppet state like Manchukuo "would result in a festering sore which will inevitably lead to future wars." Although Mr. Grew shared these view-

points, he warned Secretary Stimson that any protest from the United States concerning Japanese recognition of Manchukuo would play right into the hands of the military clique in Tokyo. Silence would pay good diplomatic dividends.[22]

But the task of silencing Stimson was as difficult as stopping the rush of waters over Niagara Falls. He was so full of righteous indignation that he had to deliver a new blast against Japan on August 8 in an address before the Council on Foreign Relations (New York City). As Grew had anticipated, the reaction in Japan to this latest Stimson attack was widespread and bitter. Its violence caused Grew to warn Stimson that "we should have our eyes open to all possible future contingencies."[23] The policy of constantly pricking Japan might eventually lead to a dangerous outburst.

On September 3, Grew sent another telegram of warning. The Japanese Government firmly intended to see "the Manchuria venture through." The Japanese public was convinced that the "whole course of action in Manchuria is one of supreme and vital national interest," and it was determined to meet, if necessary with arms, "all opposition."[24] After sending this telegram to the Department of State, Grew confided to his Diary that Japanese resentment was really focused upon only one American—Secretary Stimson. Everyone he met in Japan was

[22] Ambassador Grew to Secretary Stimson, Tokyo, July 16, 1932. Foreign Relations: Japan, 1931–1941, I, 93–95. On June 21, 1932, Viscount Ishii had made a speech before the America-Japan Society of Tokyo in which he gave assurances that Japan would leave "no stone unturned in order to remove all possible causes of friction with her great neighbor." Shanghai Evening Post and Mercury, June 21, 1932.
[23] Ambassador Grew to Secretary Stimson, Tokyo, August 13, 1932. Foreign Relations: Japan, 1931–1941, I, 100.
[24] Ambassador Grew to Secretary Stimson, Tokyo, September 3, 1932. Ibid., p. 102.

"thoroughly friendly" and his personal relations with Japanese officials were of "the best." But Stimson had enraged all Japan with his policy of constant hostile pressure.[25] It was not hard for a diplomat to see the inevitable result of these tactics.

In some circles in Japan the hope was expressed that a change in the Administration in Washington would bring a change in Far Eastern policy. But Stimson still had some six months to serve as Secretary of State, and there was the ominous possibility that during the period he would so firmly fix the pattern of policy that a new Secretary would be unable to alter it. Of one thing everyone in Japan could be certain—Stimson would not recede from the stand he had taken, no matter what the result. America might not be pushed to the point of actual conflict with Japan, but the road to war would be wide open and an invitation to hostilities would be ready for the anxious consideration of the President-elect.

In order to make sure that this invitation would be no empty affair, Stimson had consented to have Major General Frank R. McCoy serve as a member of the Lytton Commission of Enquiry. If this commission denounced Japanese aggression in North China in acidulous terms, General McCoy would bear a portion of the responsibility for such an indictment.

On October 1, 1932, the report of the Lytton Commission was published in Geneva. It made some interesting admissions. The rapid growth of the Communist Party was briefly described and the inability of Chiang Kai-shek to suppress it was clearly indicated.[26] But nothing was said about Soviet infiltration of Sinkiang and the absorption of Outer Mongolia. Japan was to be the culprit in China, not Russia. In order to prove this point the report expressed in very positive terms the belief that Japan made use of the Mukden Incident of September 18 to carry out a far-reaching plan of expansion in North China. It was admitted that Japan had "special interests" in Manchuria but these interests did not justify the erection of a semi-independent state like Manchukuo which would be under Japanese control. The report therefore recommended that Manchuria should enjoy "a large measure of autonomy" consistent "with the sovereignty and administrative integrity of China."[27]

The report mentioned the fact that the Japanese had erected the new state of Manchukuo on March 9, 1932, and had installed Henry Pu yi, the boy Emperor of China, as the regent. It did not indicate who was to dethrone the regent or who was to assume the grave responsibility of pushing the large Japanese Army out of Manchukuo and thus permit Manchuria to resume its former status. Indirectly, this assertion of continued Chinese sovereignty over the Three Provinces was an endorsement of the Stimson nonrecognition principle. The commission conveniently closed its eyes to the fact of Japanese control over Manchukuo and assumed that the farce of nonrecognition would bring Japan to heel. It was a little shocked when Japan formally recognized Manchukuo on September 15, and Secretary Stimson felt outraged at this defiance of his doctrine.

Two months later (November 19) Matsuoka, the head of the Japanese delegation at Geneva, whispered some warning words to Hugh Wilson and Norman

[25] Joseph C. Grew, *Ten Years in Japan* (New York, 1944), p. 40.

[26] *Lytton Report* (Washington, 1932), pp. 20–23.

[27] *Ibid.,* p. 130.

Davis. The hostility of the Japanese public toward the United States was "dangerous." There was a growing belief that several attempts had been made by the American Government to "check Japanese development in Manchuria and to get control of the railway situation in that area." The large body of influential Japanese opinion that heretofore had been friendly was "rapidly diminishing." The Japanese people had been very patient, but a point had been reached where this quality was no longer a virtue and the repressed irritation against America might break through all bonds with "suddenness and violence."[28]

Matsuoka had spent many years in the United States as a student and was known among the Japanese as "thinking and conducting himself like an American."[29] His words of warning would have had some influence upon the average Secretary of State, but Stimson refused to heed them. He carelessly boasted to Hugh Wilson that he was acquainted with the "personality and methods" of Matsuoka and had anticipated that he would assume the airs of a "clever advocate."[30] If Stimson had been blest with a more perceptive mind, he would have realized that Matsuoka was not indulging in idle threats. His words were freighted with wisdom, but Stimson still clung to the idea that he could beat the Japanese Foreign Minister into submission with the club of nonrecognition. It gave him small concern if the Foreign Minister squirmed under this punishment and if the Japanese press grew violent in its denunciations of his

policy. The Japanese would have to take their medicine no matter how bitter it tasted. . . .

In the meantime the League of Nations was giving extended consideration to the implications of the Lytton Report. On December 6 the League Assembly referred the report to a Committee of Nineteen. The representatives of several small nations on this committee were profoundly provoked with Japan because of her military operations in Manchuria. They made up for their military weakness in cascades of strong words of criticism. Stimson's quick ear caught these caustic accents and he repeated them to the Japanese Ambassador. On January 5, 1933, he talked with Debuchi, and after reviewing Japanese disregard of certain treaty obligations, he acidly observed that really there was "no other course" for Japan to follow but "to get out of the League of Nations and the Kellogg Pact."[31]

After reading this stiff lecture to the Japanese Ambassador, Stimson found time to visit Hyde Park on January 9 where he found President-elect Roosevelt in a very receptive mood. He had no trouble in convincing Roosevelt that the Stimson doctrine should be one of the pillars of the foreign policy of the new Administration. Three days later he informed Ambassador Debuchi that the President-elect would adhere to the Stimson policy.[32] On January 16 this news was sent to our diplomatic representatives abroad, and on the following day Roosevelt, at a press conference at Hyde Park, insisted that America must stand

[28] Secretary Stimson to Ambassador Grew, Washington, November 21, 1932. *Japan and the United States: 1931–1941*, I, 104–5.
[29] Frederick Moore, *With Japan's Leaders* (New York, 1942), pp. 130–31.
[30] Secretary Stimson to Hugh Wilson, November 21, 1932. *Japan and the United States, 1931–1941*, I, 105.

[31] Conversation between Secretary Stimson and Ambassador Debuchi, January 5, 1933. 793.94/5709, *Confidential file*, MS, Department of State.
[32] Conversation between Secretary Stimson and Ambassador Debuchi, January 12, 1933. *Japan and the United States, 1931–1941*, I, 108–9.

behind the principle of the "sanctity of treaties."[33] Party lines in America had disappeared when it came to imposing discipline upon Japan. . . .

Even if Secretary Stimson had been sincere in his desire to make some gesture of conciliation towards Japan, it was apparent that time was against him. In a few weeks the Roosevelt Administration would take office and it would be most unusual for an outgoing Secretary of State to take a major diplomatic step which might not be in complete agreement with the policy already outlined by his successor in office after March 4, 1933. At any rate Stimson did nothing to conciliate Japanese statesmen who were now determined to take some radical action at Geneva. The Roosevelt statement at Hyde Park on January 17 in favor of the "sanctity of treaties" failed to make much of an impression upon them. They knew that the British and French empires had been built by the blood, sweat, and tears of millions of persons in conquered countries. Why all this sudden show of international virtue? As Matsuoka sagely remarked: "The Western Powers taught the Japanese the game of poker but after acquiring most of the chips they pronounced the game immoral and took up contract bridge."[34] It was obvious to most Japanese statesmen that the conscience of the Western powers barked only at strangers.

Matsuoka Marches Out of the League

At Geneva, Matsuoka was not inclined to listen to lectures in the League Assembly on public morals, and Ambassador Grew on February 23, 1933, informed Secretary Stimson that the Japanese Cabinet was in entire agreement with the viewpoint of their chief delegate. They regarded their position in Manchuria as an essential link in the "life line" of the Japanese Empire. They were determined to fight rather than yield to League pressure.[35] In the face of this resolute Japanese attitude, the League went ahead and on February 24 it formally approved by an overwhelming vote the report of the Committee of Nineteen which had implemented the Lytton Report.[36]

This critical action on the part of the Assembly of the League of Nations provoked an immediate response from Matsuoka. After gravely stating that his government had "reached the limit of its endeavors to co-operate with the League," he marched stiffly from the hall of the Assembly. . . .

Hugh Wilson, representing the United States, was also in the Assembly as Matsuoka walked out. Like Frederick Moore he also realized that a crisis had been reached in world politics, and this crisis he knew had been precipitated by Stimson's nonrecognition policy. In his memoirs, Wilson tells the story of that fateful march of Matsuoka:

The final session of the Assembly remains indelibly printed on my mind. . . . Matsuoka's speech on that day in the Assembly was delivered with a passionate conviction far removed from his usual businesslike

[33] *New York Times*, January 18, 1933. Stimson had already assured the British Foreign Secretary, Sir John Simon, that the President-elect was committed to the Stimson doctrine. Sir John replied, January 14, that the British Government would adhere to the same doctrine. *Foreign Relations, 1933*, III, 89.
[34] Moore, *op. cit.*, pp. 38–39.

[35] *Japan and the United States: 1931–1941*, I, 110–12. On February 7, 1933, with his tongue in his cheek, Stimson instructed Hugh Wilson, United States Minister at Geneva, to make it clear that he was not in any way attempting "to guide or to influence or prejudice the League in its deliberations." *Foreign Relations, 1933*, III, 153.
[36] Russell M. Cooper, *American Consultation in World Affairs*, pp. 268–69.

manner. He pointed out the danger of pil-
lorying a great nation. He warned that the
Assembly was driving Japan from its friend-
ship with the West toward an inevitable
development of a self-sustaining, uniquely
Eastern position. . . . For the first time the
gravest doubts arose as to the wisdom of the
course which the Assembly and my country
were pursuing. I began to have a conception
of the rancor and resentment that public
condemnation could bring upon a proud and
powerful people, and I began to question,
and still do question whether such treatment
is wise. . . . Condemnation creates a community of the damned who are forced outside the pale, who have nothing to lose by
the violation of all laws of order and international good faith. . . . Not only did such
doubts regarding arraignment arise in me,
but for the first time I began to question the
non-recognition policy. More and more as I
thought it over I became conscious that we
had entered a dead-end street.[37]

It was apparent to seasoned diplomats
that the manner in which Stimson endeavored to apply the nonrecognition
formula was so provocative that war and
not peace would be the result of his
efforts. . . .

. . . On his way home from the debacle
at Geneva, Matsuoka passed through the
United States and hoped to have a conference with President Roosevelt. When
this news came to the Department of
State, Mr. Hornbeck immediately wrote
a memorandum indicating that it "would
be undesirable to have the new President
grant Mr. Matsuoka an interview." If
he (Matsuoka) were "to speak with the
President it would be only natural for
the public to assume that Matsuoka had
endeavored to convince the President of
the justice of the Japanese case."[38] For

some reason that is not clear, Mr. Hornbeck believed that the American public
should not be placed under the strain of
having to follow the arguments of Matsuoka. There was a chance that they
might be too cogent and thus defeat the
repressive policy of the Department of
State. As a result of Mr. Hornbeck's
advice, Matsuoka did not have an opportunity to present in private the case of
Japan relative to Manchukuo. . . .

The Japanese press also expressed an
ardent desire that the Roosevelt Administration would take an understanding
view of the Manchurian situation and
thereby lay the basis for "a restoration
of friendly relations between the two
nations." Matsuoka himself was quite
optimistic with reference to Japanese-
American relations. He thought that all
talk of war between the two countries
was "ridiculous." If Japan went to war
in the near future, it would be with
Soviet Russia, and Matsuoka expressed
the view that in that event "he would
not be surprised to see the United States
on Japan's side."

There was no doubt that Japan had
no wish for a war with the United States.
Matsuoka was correct in his belief that
the logical opponent for Japan in her
next war would be Russia, but logic was
not the basis for the foreign policy of the
Roosevelt Administration. The wish that
was closest to Stalin's heart was to involve Japan and the United States in a
war that would remove the Japanese barrier that prevented the Red tide from

---

[37] Hugh R. Wilson, *Diplomat Between Wars*
(New York, 1941), pp. 279–81.
[38] Memorandum by Mr. Hornbeck, Division of
Far Eastern Affairs, February 28, 1933. 811.4611

Japan/24, MS, Department of State. On March
31, 1933, Matsuoka had a brief interview with
Secretary Hull. He was "very affable" and
"urged that Japan be given time in which to
make herself better understood." With reference
to this conversation, Mr. Hull remarks: "I was
courteous but virtually silent while he was offering these parting remarks." *Foreign Relations,
1933*, p. 264.

overflowing the wide plains of China. The way that wish was gratified is the story of the succeeding chapters on Japanese-American relations. . . .

Japan Promotes Autonomy Movement in North China

It had been very clear to Theodore Roosevelt during his administration as President that Japan regarded Manchuria as a bulwark of defense and as the keystone in the economic structure of the empire. Japan could not retire from her position in that province and any attempt to force her withdrawal would lead to open warfare. President Franklin D. Roosevelt and Secretary Hull by adopting the Stimson formula of nonrecognition had opened a Pandora's box of troubles in the Far East. When they applied the formula to Japan and remained silent concerning Russia's absorption of Outer Mongolia, they emptied every evil in the box and led them to stalk along the Manchurian frontier stirring up discontent.

Chaos and communism are close companions and as Japan looked over the unsettled condition of affairs in North China, it was apparent that Russian agents were busily at work in fomenting discord. They would turn the peasants against the tottering regime of Chiang Kai-shek, and when the fires of revolution had destroyed the weak fabric of the Nationalist Government, communist armies under Mao Tse-tung or Chu Teh would quickly extinguish them under a heavy iron curtain. The formula was simple and very effective. If Japan remained inactive in North China, it would not be long before Manchuria and Korea would be closely besieged by great masses of fanatical Reds. Japan must either extend her frontiers in China or see her troops pushed into the sea.

Soviet Russia Promotes a War between China and Japan

It is apparent from the diplomatic correspondence that came to the Department of State from Nanking and Tokyo that in the summer of 1937 many Chinese officials were spoiling for a fight between Japan and China. In June 1937, Mr. Andrews, second secretary of the American Embassy in Tokyo, had a conversation with Dr. Mar who held a similar position in the Chinese Embassy. After Ambassador Grew read a report of this conversation he noted that Dr. Mar's attitude was "one of truculence and undue optimism, thus reflecting the enhanced sense of security that has been developed in a section of Chinese officialdom as a consequence of the development of the past year." China, and not Japan, was ready for the outbreak of hostilities.

In China the Japanese Ambassador kept speaking in a conciliatory vein which stressed the idea that "the time would come when there would be 'understandings' between China and Japan." As a result of these pacific words Mr. Gauss, the American Consul-General at Shanghai, reported that in informed quarters it was believed that "the Japanese are unlikely to display a strong attitude or to take any aggressive measures in North China while the question of an Anglo-Japanese understanding is being explored."

It is evident that many foreign observers in June–July 1937 regarded an outbreak of war between China and Japan as quite improbable. The Konoye Ministry seemed intent upon carrying out the pacific policy of the preceding administrations. It was with distinct surprise, therefore, that the governments of the major powers heard that armed hostilities had taken place near Peiping. On the night of July 7, in the vicinity of the famous Marco Polo bridge, some Japanese troops became involved in a sharp fight with some units of the Chinese Twenty-ninth Army. A new drama that would end on a curtain line announcing Russian domination of the Far East had opened with an ominous fanfare. The whole world became an interested audience with few of the spectators realizing that the progress of the play was pointed towards a Russian conclusion. Chinese, Japanese, and Americans would move across the Far Eastern stage in intricate patterns that finally proclaimed a definite Muscovite motif. The Moscow theater never staged a more effective puppet show. . . .

Japanese military authorities did not at first appear to realize the strength of this tie between the Communists and the Nationalists, and they hoped for an early settlement of the clash on the night of July 7. Some of them were inclined to believe that "the firing by Chinese troops which started the incident was not premeditated."[39] This conciliatory attitude led to the agreement of July 11 which was formally signed by General Chang on the nineteenth. Its terms were mild. There would be an apology and some punishment for the Chinese captain responsible for the outbreak of hostilities. There would also be assurances for the future which provided for the voluntary retirement of Chinese officials in North China who impeded Sino-Japanese cooperation and the expulsion of the communistic elements from the Peiping district.[40]

On July 12 the Japanese Ambassador (Saito) had a long conversation with Secretary Hull during the course of which he explained the policy of the Foreign Office. At the conclusion of Saito's remarks, Hull expressed his approval of Japanese efforts "to work out a friendly settlement" of the incident.[41] On the following day Ambassador Grew informed the Department of State that he believed that "if some way of avoiding general hostilities without losing face could be found, the Japanese Government might possibly still be pleased to find this way.[42]

It seemed to Mr. Hornbeck that the Japanese Foreign Office was taking the position that conversations should not be held by representatives of the Chinese and Japanese governments "but between Japanese officials in North China and the local Chinese officials on the theory that North China is a political entity separate from the authority and control of the Chinese (Nanking) Government." It was his opinion that the American Government should "make no approach to either the Chinese or the Japanese authorities and make no public comment."[43]

Secretary Hull followed this advice. On the evening of July 13 he summoned Ambassador Saito to his apartment in the Carlton Hotel and frankly informed him that the American Government was "paramountly concerned in the preservation of peace." Because of this fact it would confine its utterances "to phrases entirely within range of its impartial, friendly attitude towards all alike." Its action would "stop entirely short of any question or phase of mediation."[44]

[39] Walter H. Mallory, "Japan Attacks, China Resists," Foreign Affairs, XVI (October 1937), 129–33.
[40] Memorandum by the ambassador in Japan (Grew), Tokyo, July 22, 1937. United States and Japan, 1931–1941, I, 333–34.

[41] Memorandum by Secretary Hull, July 12, 1937. Ibid., pp. 316–18.
[42] Ambassador Grew to Secretary Hull, Tokyo, July 13, 1937. Ibid., pp. 319–20.
[43] Memorandum by Mr. Hornbeck, July 13, 1937. 793.94/8737, 8922, MS, Department of State.

This "hands off" attitude would continue to be observed by the Department of State if no general war followed the clash at Peiping. In the event of long-continued hostilities tremendous pressure would be exerted upon Secretary Hull to undertake some form of mediation. But in the early days of July 1937 there still seemed some hope for peace. It was true, however, that the action of the Chinese Nationalist Government in disavowing the agreement of July 11 was causing deep concern in the minds of many observers. When this disavowal was followed by the dispatch of "a large body of troops" to the Peiping area, it was obvious that a crisis had arrived.[45]. . .

The British Foreign Office favored a "combined Anglo-American démarche" in Tokyo and Nanking rather than an invocation of the Nine-Power Treaty, and Foreign Secretary Eden suggested this to Ambassador Bingham. From Tokyo, Ambassador Grew expressed a strong dissent from this view. He could see "no reason why we should take action."[46] He also indicated that in Japan the unanimity of opinion relative to the situation in North China was "striking." It was not "a case of unwilling deference by the Government to military initiative. The Cabinet enjoys high prestige, is wholly in command and lends full support to steps recently taken by the Japanese Army in North China. . . . At no time during the period of my assignment at this post have I observed indications of so strong and unanimous a determination on the part of the Japanese Government to resist even at the cost of extensive hostilities any movement which might tend to weaken the position of Japan in North China." Mr. Grew also remarked that there was not sufficient evidence to justify the hypothesis that "either the Japanese Government or the Army deliberately engineered the incident in order to force a 'show down.' " . . .[47]

On July 16, Ambassador Grew reported from Tokyo that "the steady development of plans of the Chinese Government to mobilize its forces and to concentrate them in North China was the principal cause for the decision taken yesterday by the Japanese Government to send reinforcements from Japan to North China."

        *   *   *

The communist menace in China gave Secretary Hull little concern. He was now thoroughly aroused over reports of indiscriminate bombings in China by the Japanese. In a long instruction to Ambassador Grew he spoke his mind very plainly. It appeared to him that Japanese unresponsiveness to American protests against bombings showed that the Japanese Government did not set a high value upon American efforts "to cultivate good will, confidence, and stability in general." If the Japanese Government would just follow the high principles enunciated by the American Government on July 16 the situation in the Far East would probably improve. While the American Government had endeavored to follow an "absolutely impartial course" during the current crisis in China, the actions of the Japanese armed forces had shocked American opinion. It would be expedient for the Japanese Government

---

[44] Memorandum by Secretary Hull, July 13, 1937. *United States and Japan, 1931–1941*, I, 320–22.

[45] Ambassador Grew to Secretary Hull, Tokyo, July 13, 1937. 793.94/8741, MS, Department of State.

[46] Ambassador Grew to Secretary Hull, Tokyo, July 13, 1937. 793.94/8742, MS, Department of State.

[47] Ambassador Grew to Secretary Hull, Tokyo, July 13, 1937. 793.94/8745, MS, Department of State.

to keep in mind that their course in China was looked upon in America with the same degree of disapproval that it had evoked in Britain. American public opinion "has been outraged by the methods and strategy employed by the combatants, particularly by the Japanese military, and has become gradually more critical of Japan." It was high time the Japanese Government gave heed to the principles so often expressed by the Department of State.[48]

It is evident that the statement of American principles by Secretary Hull on July 16 was a verbal bombshell directed against Japan. All talk of an "absolutely impartial course" towards China and Japan during the July crisis was mere diplomatic eyewash which no realistic statesmen took seriously. Hull was definitely antagonistic towards Japan, and his statement of July 16 was a prelude to the quarantine speech of President Roosevelt on October 5....

The quarantine speech of October 5 had many macabre overtones designed to frighten the American people. It indicated that large portions of the world were experiencing a "reign of terror," and that the "landmarks and traditions which have marked the progress of civilization toward a condition of law, order and justice" were being "wiped away." "Innocent peoples and nations" were being "cruelly sacrificed to a greed for power and supremacy" which was "devoid of all sense of justice and humane consideration." If this sad condition of affairs existed in other parts of the world it was vain for anyone to "imagine that America will escape, that it may expect mercy, that this Western Hemisphere will not be attacked, and that it will continue

tranquilly and peacefully to carry on the ethics and the arts of civilization."

Newspapers of a one-world persuasion sprang to the President's support. The New York Times and the World-Telegram promptly attacked the "unrealities of isolation,"[49] while the New York Daily News suggested a long-range Anglo-American naval blockade of Japan if that nation were to overrun China and threaten the interests of the Western powers."[50]

Some papers advocated an economic boycott as a means to bring Japan to reason. The Washington Post urged that America "immediately cease to buy Japanese goods,"[51] and this opinion was strongly seconded by the Washington Evening Star[52] and the Rochester Democrat and Chronicle.[53] The Atlanta Constitution expressed the emphatic opinion that "war-diseased nations must be quarantined,"[54] and the Birmingham News[55] and the Raleigh News and Observer[56] joined the chorus. In the Middle West the Chicago Daily News,[57] the St. Louis Globe-Democrat,[58] and the Cincinnati Enquirer[59] expressed agreement with the "general principles" of the President's address. On the Pacific Coast the San Francisco Chronicle,[60] the Los Angeles Times,[61] and the Portland Morning Oregonian[62] adopted a favorable attitude.

But there was a large legion of newspapers that rejected any thought of eco-

[48] Secretary Hull to Ambassador Grew, September 2, 1937. United States and Japan, 1931–1941, I, 361–64.

[49] October 6, 8, 1937.
[50] October 3, 7, 1937.
[51] October 8, 1937.
[52] October 6, 7, 1937.
[53] October 6, 1937.
[54] October 7, 1937.
[55] October 6, 11, 1937.
[56] October 6, 8, 1937.
[57] October 6, 8, 1937.
[58] October 15, 1937.
[59] October 7, 8, 1937.
[60] October 6, 1937.
[61] October 6, 7, 1937.
[62] October 6, 1937.

nomic sanctions against Japan. Such action would lead to war. The *New York Herald Tribune* believed that the President's speech had been based upon the "identical sands of confusion, emotion and wishful thinking which so tragically engulfed Mr. Wilson's great vision."[63] The New York *Sun* warned the President that American public opinion would not approve any policy of "pulling chestnuts out of the fire for any association of foreign nations."[64] The *Boston Herald* boldly declared that "Americans must not embark on another costly attempt to reform the world,"[65] while even the staunchly Democratic *Boston Post* cried out in protest: "He [the President] must know that the American people are in no mood for a crusade."[66]

The *Chicago Tribune* was openly hostile to any threat of a boycott against Japan. Economic sanctions would lead America down the road to war.[67] The *Detroit Free Press* voiced the opinion that there was no "adequate reason for remarks that were evangelistic rather than statesmanlike, and were manifestly designed to stir emotions rather than provoke careful thought."[68] The *Milwaukee Journal* remarked that a boycott is a "first cousin to outright war,"[69] and the Spokane *Spokesman-Review* stated ominously that the President's Chicago address "approximated a declaration of war."[70]

The columnists were divided in their opinions of the Chicago address. Boake Carter was fearful that the President suffered from the "disease of moral fervor

for reform."[71] Paul Mallon regarded the address as a clever move to divert attention from the unfortunate appointment of Hugo Black to the Supreme Court,[72] while General Hugh S. Johnson was worried that America, as in 1917, would play the role of "sucker."[73]

On the other hand, David Lawrence hailed the address as the "speech the whole world has been waiting for several months to hear,"[74] Dorothy Thompson was delighted that she could now envisage the end of American "neutrality,"[75] and Walter Lippmann praised the President for a much-needed clarion call to the democracies to resist aggressor nations.[76]

The Catholic press had few words of praise for the President's Chicago challenge. *America* flatly stated that the "people of the United States positively are opposed to foreign imbroglios";[77] the *Ave Maria* was filled with misgivings,[78] while Father Gillis, in the *Catholic World*, was sharply critical of any pressure in favor of American intervention in the Far East.[79]

It is interesting to note that the *Christian Century*, which reflected the Protestant viewpoint, was distinctly suspicious of the Chicago speech. In a forecast of the future it warned that if America went

[63] October 6, 8, 1937.
[64] October 6, 7, 1937.
[65] October 6, 7, 1937.
[66] October 11, 1937.
[67] October 6, 1937.
[68] October 7, 1937.
[69] October 10, 1937.
[70] October 6, 7, 1937.

[71] *Boston Daily Globe*, October 8, 1937.
[72] *Boston Herald*, October 8, 1937.
[73] *New York World-Telegram*, October 6, 1937.
[74] *Chicago Daily News*, October 7, 1937.
[75] *New York Herald Tribune*, October 10, 1937.
[76] *New York Herald Tribune*, October 16, 1937.
[77] October 16, 1937.
[78] October 23, 1937, pp. 534–35.
[79] December 1937, pp. 257–65. On October 9, 1937, Senator David I. Walsh wrote a note to Secretary Hull in which he inclosed a telegram from the Maryknoll Fathers in Japan. They deeply regretted the "recent change official attitude towards Sino-Japanese trouble," and urgently requested his influence "towards restoring previous attitude impartial tolerance as most practical policy." 793.94/10546, MS, Department of State.

to war on behalf of China the result would be a victory for Russia.[80]

This Russian angle of the situation in the Far East was clearly perceived by many observers. On October 12 the Division of Far Eastern Affairs prepared a memorandum for the use of Secretary Hull. With reference to possible economic sanctions, the memorandum asks the question whether the United States should take the lead in such a movement. In answer to this question it remarks: "It is believed that the assuming of such a position by any country would bring that country face to face with a very real hazard. . . . It seems to me [Mr. Hamilton, chief of the Division] that public opinion in the United States is definitely opposed to the United States assuming a position of leadership in the imposing of restrictive measures directed at Japan.

[80] October 20, 1937, pp. 1287–88.

Moreover it should be borne in mind that if restrictive measures should take the form of economic 'sanctions,' the United States would be called upon to carry the heaviest burden.[81] . . . If some program could be worked out which would give Japan a reasonable prospect of economic security and which would remove Japan's fear of Communism and attack from the Soviet Union, there would be removed some basic elements in the situation responsible for Japan's present imperialistic program."[82]

[81] In a letter to Mr. Hornbeck, Mr. Taneo Taketa, a representative of the South Manchuria Railway, points out the close economic ties between the United States and Japan. The South Manchuria Railway alone had purchased "far more than $100,000,000 worth of equipment from the United States." Other firms had purchased large amounts. 793.94/10708, MS, Department of State.

[82] Memorandum prepared by the Division of Far Eastern Affairs, October 12, 1937. 793.94/10706, MS, Department of State.

Herbert Feis: THE ROAD TO PEARL HARBOR

A proponent of the Roosevelt Administration, Herbert Feis is the author of the following selection from The Road to Pearl Harbor *in which he argues that Roosevelt and Hull could follow no other course in the interest of national security and morality than to oppose Japanese aggression while offering every possible incentive to Japan to forego its Axis connection. Feis contends that the Administration did all in its power to avoid war and, at least, gained time to prepare. Feis, now a member of the Institute for Advanced Study, Princeton, was actively engaged as a government adviser, served on the policy planning staff of the State Department, and has held a Guggenheim Fellowship. A Pulitzer Prize winner, he has written of the continuing diplomacy and strategy of the United States and her allies in* Churchill, Roosevelt, and Stalin; Between War and Peace; Japan Subdued; The China Tangle; *and* The Potsdam Conference.

After Our Elections: Steps towards a Concerted Program

NOVEMBER 1940; the Roosevelt administration was safely confirmed in power. It could properly construe the election result as approval of its opposition to the Axis and its support of Britain short of war. But, because of the terms in which he had expounded these policies during the campaign, the President was obliged still to move warily and on the slant. The words spoken during the election contest lived on to complicate and confine decision for the times ahead.

Americans had been told that they need not take part in the battles then being fought in Europe and Asia and that the government would not cause them to do so.[1] They had been urged to provide

weapons and resources to fend off the danger of having to go to war. British resistance, the expressed thought ran, was giving us time to become so strong that no country, or group of countries,

"I have said this before, but I shall say it again and again and again:

"Your boys are not going to be sent into any foreign wars.

"They are going into training to form a force so strong that, by its very existence, it will keep the threat of war far away from our shores.

"The purpose of our defense is defense."

It can, of course, be well argued that the question of what is or is not a "foreign war" is not to be learned from a map alone. But the manner in which it was used during the campaign seemed to give it a simple meaning of wars fought in and by foreign countries. The term was, unless I am mistaken, taken over from the opponents of intervention. A cousinly term was effectively used by Charles A. Beard in the title of a virulent article that he published in *Harper's Magazine* for September 1939, "Giddy Minds and Foreign Quarrels."

Willkie spoke in the same strain as Roosevelt; in fact he set the pace in providing assurance that the United States need not and should not enter the war. The isolationists were far more extreme, denouncing any and all acts of intervention.

[1] The most unguarded of these statements, amounting to a promise, was made by the President in a speech in Boston on October 30 when he said:

"And while I am talking to you mothers and fathers, I give you one more assurance.

Reprinted from *The Road to Pearl Harbor* by Herbert Feis by Permission of Princeton University Press, copyright 1950. Excerpted from pages 133–328.

would dare attack us. While if the Axis won, the United States would become exposed to its fury and forced to fight near or within our own land. This was a correct judgment of the meaning to us of the wars in Europe and Asia. It was a well founded basis for the program sponsored by the government and for the acceptance of the connected risks. But it left the President open to a charge of blunder or bad faith if the United States found itself at war.

The government avoided all actions which could not be construed as defensive. It continued—and it was no easy thing to do—to refuse to enter into any accord which carried an obligation to go to war. But it shaped our policies in conference with other governments and fitted its action to theirs. We were about to form a common front against Japan without admitting it or promising to maintain it by force.

Before leaving the subject, a comment may be added about the information given the American people during the months after the election—the winter of 1940–41. Some things that were done were wholly told, some vaguely told, and a few, such as naval talks and movements, were hardly told at all. The President's utterances of this period did not provide all the explanatory knowledge that could have been wanted to follow and judge American policy in action. For they were not systematic statements of the situation facing the United States and the choice before it. They were emotional appeals to the American people to hurry along their military preparations and to stand firm and hard against the Axis. They were written as such, not by essayists but by political advisers and dramatists. They were pin-pointed explosives.[2] They were exertions of leadership in behalf of measures that were secretly in the making, or rather in the taking.

*   *   *

While keeping the American fleet at American bases, while refusing to say what it would or would not do if Japan sailed into the Southwest Pacific, the American government—within a month after the elections—put together a program of subtly adjusted measures to hinder Japan.

First came the decisions in regard to aid for China in response to Chiang Kai-shek's appeals. On November 30 the President announced that we would put another 100 million dollars at his disposal. Fifty modern pursuit planes at once were promised him, with as many more as possible. Steps were taken to issue passports to American citizens who wished to go to China to serve as aviators or aviation instructors. A plan for providing China with long-range bombers so that it could hit back at Tokyo was excitedly discussed with the British and Chinese. To the chagrin of all, it was found impractical.[3] These measures were

_____

[2] To adopt a description used by Robert E. Sher-

wood—*Roosevelt and Hopkins* (New York, 1948), p. 184—who writes that Willkie's radio speeches "sounded" harsh, hurried and diffuse—short-range blasts of birdshot rather than pinpointed high explosive shells."

[3] This seems to have been inspired by a remark of the President that it would be a good thing if the Chinese could bomb Japan. Morgenthau took it up, and talked it over with Lothian and T. V. Soong who enthusiastically cabled Chiang Kai-shek. Hull said he was for it, but it might occur to skeptical spirits who knew him that he saw no need to catch that arrow in his hand since it would soon fall to earth. Chiang Kai-shek answered that he would carry out the plan, provided the United States supplied not only the bombers but escort planes and the necessary ground organization. We, of course, had none of these to spare; the bombers would have had to be taken from the allotments destined for Britain, Hawaii, and the Philippines. The idea was dropped at a meeting on December 23, when

the outcome of a tense effort to make sure that the Chiang Kai-shek regime would be able and willing to keep in the fight.

Ships and planes were sent out to the Philippines. Six submarines went, with more to follow. Plans were made to assemble the whole Asiatic fleet at Manila and to increase its size. Hull urged that the Navy send as well a whole squadron of cruisers to southernmost Philippine ports. The President was briefly for this, but changed his mind. He also wanted to publish the news of our naval movements, but he took Hull's advice to let them become known by reports that were certain to seep out, as the ships were seen. A public announcement, he thought, might cause trouble of two kinds: objection within the United States which would lessen the effect upon Japan; and excitement within Japan. Japan was not to be threatened publicly, but to be left guessing.

"I believed in letting them guess as to when and in what set of circumstances we would fight. While Japan continued to guess, we continued to get ready for anything she might do."[4]

The Japanese were not the only ones compelled to guess. The British were just as uncertain. A month later Harry Hopkins from London was reporting to the President that "Eden asked me repeatedly what our country would do if Japan attacked Singapore or the Dutch East Indies, saying it was essential to their policy to know."[5]

The thought may be carried further. Not only did the British not know what we would do, but neither did Roosevelt or Hull know. Would the President ask Congress to declare war on Japan? Or would he merely take some lesser measures—such as turning submarines over to the British, or using American naval forces to maintain a patrol and convoy system in the Pacific? Or, because that might waste naval forces, would he not even do that?

He was spared the need of deciding. Most fortunately so. For grave uses for the fleet in the Atlantic loomed up more clearly than before, and a great need to face Hitler with unengaged forces. On December 8, Churchill, by letter, put before the President (through Hull) a lucid and compelling summary of the situation faced by Britain and of the aid it would need to carry on. Among its parts were these: "The danger of Great Britain being destroyed by a swift, overwhelming blow has for the time being very greatly receded. In its place there is a long, gradually maturing danger, less sudden and less spectacular, but equally deadly. This mortal danger is the steady and increasing diminution of sea tonnage. . . . The decision for 1941 lies upon the seas. Unless we can establish our ability to feed this island, to import the munitions of all kinds which we need, unless we can move our armies to the various theatres where Hitler and his confederate Mussolini must be met, and maintain them there . . . we may fall by the way, and the time needed by the United States to complete her defensive preparations may not be forthcoming. It is, therefore, in shipping and in the power to transport across the oceans, particularly the Atlantic Ocean, that in 1941 the crunch of the whole war will be found."[6]

In drafting this, Churchill had before him Stark's memo of November 12. A copy had been sent on to him by the Brit-

---

General Marshall demonstrated how impractical it was. Morgenthau diary, entries for December 3, 7, 8, 10, 18, 20, 22, and 23, 1940.
[4] Hull, *op. cit.*, I, 915.
[5] Sherwood, *op. cit.*, p. 259.

[6] Winston S. Churchill, *Their Finest Hour* (Boston, 1949), p. 560.

ish naval representative in Washington, along with Stark's remark that it would be useful if the Prime Minister endorsed the basic suggestions therein contained. The advice was taken to heart. The Prime Minister's analysis left no doubt that the United States would have to do more than it had done.

While the President was still in the Caribbean, the problem drew together Hull, Knox, Stimson, Stark, and Marshall. They hunted for the response that would be sufficient yet possible. All agreed with the comment that Stimson wrote in his diary while these talks were on: "It is very apparent that nothing will save Great Britain from the starvation of her supplies, which Stark estimates will necessarily take place in six months, except assistance from us by convoy in the Atlantic . . ."[7] When Stimson so proposed in the cabinet (on December 19), "The President said he hadn't quite reached that yet."[8]

But, short of that, the resolve emerged from these December conferences to extend American naval protection over the Atlantic as far and as fast as might be necessary, and in the face of any risks of fighting at sea. This was enough (though not the sole) reason for refusing to promise to join the defense of Singapore and the Indies; enough reason why the President could not know or tell what he might do if Japan attacked them. A season was ahead in which the forces of the Allies were to be most wanly stretched. . . .

In the disturbed realm of diplomacy which the United States and Japan had entered, the language used is in part symbolic, in part spoken. Battleships and economic controls are the symbol of power in reserve, symbols used to give

edge to verbal warnings, a way of saying "Do you see what I mean?" without saying it. But at the same time the American government was giving secret spoken warnings to Japan.

Dooman, the experienced Counselor of the American Embassy in Tokyo, had been on leave in the United States. He was known by the Japanese to be a firm and straightforward friend. So it was thought that his report of the state of American opinion might be accepted as advice rather than as a threat. On February 14 (Tokyo time) he put before Ohashi, the Vice-Minister for Foreign Affairs, the "philosophy" of the American position. The Vice-Minister was told that the American people were determined to support Britain even at the risk of war; that if Japan or any other country menaced that effort it "would have to expect to come into conflict with the United States"; that if Japan were to occupy Dutch or British areas in the Pacific it would create havoc with the British situation in the war; and that the United States had abstained from an oil embargo in order not to impel Japan to create a situation that could only lead to the most serious outcome.

On the same date, Febuary 14 (Washington time), the President had his first talk with the new Japanese Ambassador, Admiral Nomura. He made no such blunt affirmations. By being affable and eager, the President sought to show that he wished peace, not war. He spoke as though the danger of war lay in a chance error or incident rather than because of any basic clash of interest. The purpose was to encourage the Japanese government to talk with us. If, as was thought, and correctly thought, in Washington, there was still a division of opinion in the Japanese government, an engagement to

---

[7] Stimson diary, entry for December 16, 1940.
[8] *Ibid.*, entry for December 19, 1940.

talk with us would help the proponents of peace. The light touch was chosen for heavy work, for critical work.[9]

In summary, then, American policy during this winter period of alarm (January-February) was a compound of warning gestures, slowly spreading coercion, earnest advice, and an invitation to talk.

The reports that came back from Tokyo were taken to mean that this policy was, at least for the time being, effective. Grew reported on the 18th of February that the Japanese officials were much disturbed by the reactions abroad; and that Matsuoka was being compelled again to defend himself against criticisms of the Tripartite Pact. The Japanese Foreign Office denied in a calm note on the 20th to the British that there was any basis for their alarm; nor for the warlike preparations which the British and the Americans were taking to meet unreal contingencies in the South Seas.

On February 20, or thereabouts, it became confirmed that Matsuoka was about to leave for Moscow, Berlin, and Rome. "For the purpose," Churchill informed the President, "of covering the failure of action against us."[10] This was not an adequate explanation. But about the direction of Matsuoka's mind at any given moment any guess seemed to be as good as another—so like a twisted rope was

he. As when told by Grew that everything that Dooman had said to Ohashi had his (Grew's) entire concurrence and approval, he answered that he entirely agreed with what Dooman had said.[11] To Craigie at about the same time he said that Japan's motto was "No conquest, no oppression, no exploitation."

Matsuoka's words were not trusted. But the allowance of time was a great relief. And beyond that a great chance—both to strive further to avert war with Japan, and to get ready for the fight if war came. Projects for each purpose were in secret course. Two ladders were being built for history; no one knew which would be used. . . .

In weighing all that came after, these four points should be borne in mind, for they marked out the ground on which the American government stood. In some phases of the talks with Japan, it was deemed discreet to leave them in the background. But they were never forgotten. In order they were:

1. Respect for the territorial integrity and the sovereignty of each and all nations.

2. Support of the principle of non-interference in the internal affairs of other countries.

3. Support of the principle of equality, including equality of commercial opportunity.

4. Non-disturbance of the *status quo* in the Pacific except as the *status quo* may be altered by peaceful means.

The Japanese government did not want to argue principles; abstract principles, which took no account of place, time, or degree. It wanted an end to American aid to China, a lifting of the embargoes, economic independence, a commanding place in the Far East. Thus, the Japanese records verify, it studied this list of com-

---

[9] Hull's memorandum of this talk is printed in *Foreign Relations: Japan,* II, 387–89.

[10] In this message of February 20, reprinted in *Pearl Harbor Attack,* Part 19, p. 3454, Churchill attributed the postponement of the attack to fear of the United States. He was doing his best to keep the fear alive, as when on the 24th he remarked to the Japanese Ambassador in London that it would be a pity if Japan, already at war with China, should find itself at war with Great Britain and the United States. But he took occasion also to assure the Japanese government that the measures taken by Britain were only for defense, that no attack would be made upon Japan or Japanese forces.

[11] *Foreign Relations: Japan,* II, 143.

mandments glumly. They made a cavern in which Japan could become lost and delayed. But the Japanese government was to find that there was no way round them. Or, as the matter was regarded by the heads of that government (and so stated in their later defense), American insistence that Japan subscribe to these four principles was "symptomatic of a doctrinairism which was to exercise a baleful influence throughout." . . .[12]

On July 2 there came together in the presence of the Emperor the chief figures of the civil and military governments of Japan. These included the Prime Minister, Prince Konoye; the Foreign Minister, Matsuoka; the Minister for War, General Tojo; the Minister for the Navy, Admiral Oikawa; the Chief of the Army General Staff, General Sugiyama; the Chief of the Naval General Staff, Admiral Nagano; the President of the Privy Council, Hara; and the Minister for Home Affairs, Hiranuma. The plans ratified at this Imperial Conference set into determined motion the acts and responses that six months later resulted in war between Japan and the United States. The tail of the serpent wound round to its mouth.

From the text of the resolution adopted at this conference the course of events that followed can now be clearly traced. It is not very long and the reader, I think, will want to have most of it.[13]

[12] *Far East Mil. Trib.*, Defense Document No. 3100.

[13] I have selected the translation of this "Outline of the Policy of the Imperial Government in View of Present Developments" contained in the "Konoye Memoirs" (as printed in *Pearl Harbor Attack*, Part 20, pp. 4018–19), in preference to that contained in the text presented to the *International Military Tribunal* (Exh. No. 588). Between these two translations there are points of difference, both in the order of exposition and in the tone, though no basic difference in meaning. The translation presented to the *International Military Tribunal* reads as though the Japanese government were virtually determined on war with the United States, while the one herein

An Outline of the Policy of the Imperial Government in View of Present Developments

(Decision reached at the Conference held in the Imperial Presence on July 2)

I. Policy

1. The Imperial Government is determined to follow a policy which will result in the establishment of the Greater East Asia Co-Prosperity Sphere and world peace, no matter what international developments take place.

2. The Imperial Government will continue its effort to effect a settlement of the China Incident and seek to establish a solid basis for the security and preservation of the nation. This will involve an advance into the southern regions and, depending on future developments, a settlement of the Soviet Question as well.

3. The Imperial Government will carry out the above program no matter what obstacles may be encountered.

II. Summary

1. Steps will be taken to bring pressure on the Chiang Regime from the southern approaches in order to bring about its surrender. Whenever demanded by future developments the rights of a belligerent will be resorted to against Chungking and hostile concessions taken over.

2. In order to guarantee national security and preservation, the Imperial Government will continue all necessary diplomatic negotiations with reference to the southern regions and also carry out various other plans as may be necessary. In case the diplomatic negotiations break down, preparations for a war with England and America will also be carried forward. First of all, the plans which have been laid with reference to French Indo-China and Thai will be prosecuted, with a view to consolidating our position in the southern territories.

In carrying out the plans outlined in the

used seems to regard that event as a possibility against which Japan was to prepare but still seek to avoid.

foregoing article, we will not be deterred by the possibility of being involved in a war with England and America.

3. Our attitude with reference to the German-Soviet War will be based on the spirit of the Tri-Partite Pact. However, we will not enter the conflict for some time but will steadily proceed with military preparations against the Soviet and decide our final attitude independently. At the same time, we will continue carefully correlated activities in the diplomatic field.

. . . In case the German-Soviet War should develop to our advantage, we will make use of our military strength, settle the Soviet question and guarantee the safety of our northern borders. . . .

4. In carrying out the preceding article all plans, especially the use of armed forces, will be carried out in such a way as to place no serious obstacles in the path of our basic military preparations for a war with England and America.

5. In case all diplomatic means fail to prevent the entrance of America into the European War, we will proceed in harmony with our obligations under the Tri-Partite Pact. However, with reference to the time and method of employing our armed forces we will take independent action.

6. We will immediately turn our attention to placing the nation on a war basis and will take special measures to strengthen the defenses of the nation.

7. Concrete plans covering this program will be drawn up separately.

The main lines of this policy were set and most stubbornly held by the forces who spoke through General Tojo. They did not get their whole way, but a ruinous share of it. They thought that if Japan acquired a self-sufficient base of operation in the south it could wear down China, and stand, if need be, a long war against Britain and the United States. The Army and Navy were to get ready for such a war. But the hope remained that it would not have to be fought. It was expected that if Germany defeated Russia, the United States and Britain would give way; that they would allow Japan to establish the New Order in East Asia at the expense of others.

To Matsuoka this course of action was a rebuff and a mistake. But he buoyed himself up with the belief that his views would prevail later. Thus he busied himself with excuses, assuring Ribbentrop that Japan was preparing for all eventualities and when the time came would turn against Russia; in the meantime the advancing vigil in the Pacific was no less a contribution to the common cause.[14] To Konoye and the Imperial Household the resolution of July 2 was at least a temporary respite from the disputes with which they were surrounded. All gambled on the chance that the German armies would bring both the Soviet Union and the British down before winter came. Then there would be only one strong possible enemy left—the United States. This was the strategy that failed. But it might have won.

Japan's actions during the next few months followed this plan:

The economic resources of the country were organized for war.

The entry into Indo-China was begun. Before July ended the demands were served upon Petain, and the Japanese Navy and Army moved into Indo-China.

The Army hastened its operational plans against Malaya, Java, and other points in the Netherlands East Indies, Borneo, the Bismarck Archipelago, and the Philippines.[15]

The Navy developed corresponding plans—among them one highly secret

[14] *Ibid.*, Exh. Nos. 636, 796, 1113.

[15] Testimony of General Tanaka (Shinichi), Chief of the Operations Section, General Staff of the Army. The studies were ordered by General Sugiyama, Chief of the General Staff, with the approval of Tojo and General Muto, Chief of the (so-called) Military Affairs Bureau of the War Minister.

tactic. It began to practice the Pearl Harbor attack, conceived first in January. The fleets went into Kagoshima Bay and there the planes practiced coming in low over the mountains, dive bombing, and the use of torpedoes, specially designed for shallow waters.[16]

The Japanese government gave the government of the Soviet Union on July 2 formal assurances that it would observe the neutrality pact.[17] The size of the Kwantung Army was increased (from some 300 thousand men to about twice that number). But troops were withdrawn from the borders of Manchukuo and concentrated at interior points. Orders were given to avoid border troubles with Russian forces and compose any incidents as quickly as possible.[18] At the same time a new plan of operations against Siberia was prepared; in contrast to former ones it contemplated simultaneous attacks on several fronts.

All these items of preparation looked towards war. And yet most of the Konoye Cabinet still eagerly wished to avoid war with the United States. If persuasion and the use of the least offensive forms could keep the United States quiet, they would not be economized.[19] . . .

By July 20 "Magic," as well as other sources, supplied the answers as to whether the reformed Konoye Cabinet would renounce its attachment to Germany or its plan to occupy Indo-China. It did not intend to do either. A message which Toyoda had broadcast on July 19 (Tokyo time) to various Japanese diplomatic missions was intercepted. This stated "that although the Cabinet has changed there will be no departure from the principle that the Tripartite Pact forms the keystone of Japanese national policy." Another intercepted message of July 20 (Tokyo time) revealed that Toyoda told Kato (the Japanese Ambassador in Vichy) that the Japanese Army was ready and would advance into Indo-China on the 24th, whether or not the French government consented. . . .

We Freeze Japan's Funds

On the next day, the 24th, the radio reported that Japanese warships had appeared off Camranh Bay, and that twelve troop transports were on their way south from Hainan. . . .

At eight o'clock in the evening the President's office at Poughkeepsie passed out to the press a release which stated that, in view of the unlimited national emergency, the President was issuing an Executive Order freezing Japanese assets in the United States. "This measure," the press release continued, "in effect, brings all financial and import and export trade transactions in which Japanese interests are involved under the control of the government. . . ."[20]

The step had been taken which was to force Japan to choose between making terms with us or making war against us. No longer would the United States be providing the resources which left her better able to fight if she should so decide. . . .

. . . If Japan was to fight, the longer it waited the greater the risk that the battle

---

[16] Interrogation of Admiral Nagano, *ibid.*, Exh. No. 1127 (a).

[17] When first asked about this by the Soviet Ambassador, Smetanin, on June 25, Matsuoka evaded and left the matter doubtful. Extract from Smetanin's diary, entry for June 25, 1941, *ibid.*, Exh. No. 793.

[18] Testimony of General Tanaka.

[19] Testimony of General Tominago (Kijoji), Section Chief, War Ministry, *ibid.*, Exh. No. 705; of General Yanagita (Genzo), Chief, Army Special Service Agency, Harbin, *ibid.*, Exh. No. 723; of General Otsubo (Kazuma), Chief of Staff, Third Front of Kwantung Army, *ibid.*, Exh. No. 837.

[20] Press release issued at Poughkeepsie, N.Y., by the White House at 8 P. M., July 25, 1941.

might be lost for lack of oil or other essential raw materials. So the oil gauge influenced the time of decision.

Not only the time of decision, but the war plans. The wish to obtain economic reserves for a long war was an important factor in determining the spheres to be occupied. It was decided by Imperial Military Headquarters that to be sure of enough oil, rubber, rice, bauxite, iron ore, it was necessary to get swift control of Java, Sumatra, Borneo, and Malaya. In order to effect the occupation and protect the transport lines to Japan, it was necessary to expel the United States from the Philippines, Guam, and Wake, and Britain from Singapore. Thus it can be said that the points of attack and occupation were settled by placing these vital raw material needs alongside of the estimate of Japan's military means. And having settled these, the question of the weather entered in to hurry the final action.[21]

The Army and Navy feared even to see two, three, or four *months* elapse. For on their strategic calendar October and November were the best months for landing operations. December was possible but difficult, January or later, impossible.[22] If the plan were to include an attack on Pearl Harbor by the Great Circle Route,

navigational and weather conditions would, it was judged, become unfavorable after January.[23] Furthermore the sooner the southern operations were under way, the less the chance that the Soviet Union could attack from the north; if they could be completed before the end of winter, that danger need not be feared.[24]

Thus, leaving Konoye to go on with his talks with the United States, the Army and Navy threw themselves at once into the plans for action. The Operations Section of the Army began to get ready to capture Malaya, Java, Borneo, the Bismarck Archipelago, the Indies, and the Philippines; it was to be fully ready by the end of October. The Navy finished its war games. These included the surprise attack on Pearl Harbor and the American fleet there. At the end of the games the two general staffs conferred on the result and found it satisfactory.[25]

By the end of September these steps towards war—if diplomacy should fail—were well under way. Still Konoye and Toyoda found themselves reading the unchanging reports of American resistance. The President was still in the White House—planning to go no further than Warm Springs. Hull and his draftsmen

---

[21] This brief comment on the way in which the wish to obtain economic reserves affected the plans with which Japan began the war is drawn from several studies made available to me by the Military Intelligence Division of the Supreme Headquarters of the Allied Command in Tokyo; especially the information furnished by Colonel Hattori (Takushiro), former Chief of the Operations Section of the General Staff of the Japanese Army. It corresponds also to the explanations of Admiral Toyoda (Soemu), former Commanding Officer, Kure Naval District.

[22] Tojo deposition, *Far East Mil. Trib.*, Exh. No. 3655. As stated by Admiral Shimada, Minister of the Navy, in his deposition, Exh. No. 3565: "With the advent of December, northeasterly monsoons would blow with force in the Formosan Straits, the Philippines, and Malayan areas rendering military operations difficult."

[23] This forecast of weather conditions was borne out by the event—in early December. "The start (for the attack on Pearl Harbor) was from Saeki, the training harbor, about November 17, 1941; then north and across the Pacific, just south of the Aleutians, then south to Pearl Harbor. We had studied this route for a long time. Upon returning we suffered from heavy seas and strong winds." Interrogation of Captain Watanabe, on Admiral Yamamoto's staff.

[24] As stated by General Tojo in his defense deposition, and by Colonel Hattori in his study for the Supreme Command of the Allied Powers.

[25] See evidence of records of Admiral Nagano and Admiral Yamamoto, Commander in Chief of the Combined Fleet, *ibid.*, Exh. Nos. 1126 and 1127. For interesting details, see Captain Ellis M. Zacharias, *Secret Missions* (New York [1946]), pp. 243, *et seq.*

were still dissecting every document which came from Tokyo with the scalpel of mistrust. In his apartment in the Wardman Park Hotel there seemed to be no sense of hurry. No calendar hung there with October ringed in red.

Time had become the meter of strategy for both governments. But one did not mind its passing, while the other was crazed by the tick of the clock. . . .

The world may long wonder what would have happened had the President agreed then to meet with Konoye. Grew and Dooman, at the time and later, had a sense that the refusal was a sad error. To them it seemed that the American government had missed a real chance to lead Japan back to peaceful ways. Konoye, they thought, was sincere in his acceptance of those principles of international conduct for which the American government stood, and with the support of the Emperor would be able to carry through his promises. In words which Grew confided to his diary:

It is my belief that the Emperor, the Government of Prince Konoye and the militant leaders of Japan (the leaders then in control) had come to accept the status of the conflict in China, in conjunction with our freezing measures and Japan's economic condition as evidence of failure or comparative incapacity to succeed.

Our attitude, he thought and others since have thought the same), showed a lack both of insight and suppleness, if not of desire. The mistake sprang, in this view, from failure to appreciate why Konoye could not be as clear and conclusive as the American government wished; and to admit that Japan could correct its course only in a gradual and orderly way. Wise American statesmanship, thus, would have bartered adjustment for adjustment, agreeing to relax our economic restraints little by little as Japan, little by little, went our way. Instead, the judgment ends, it was dull and inflexible. By insisting that Japan promise in black and white, then and there, to conform to every American requirement, it made Konoye's task impossible.

It will be always possible to think that Grew was correct; that the authorities in Washington were too close to their texts and too soaked in their disbelief to perceive what he saw. That the American government was as stern as a righteous schoolmaster cannot be denied. Nor that it was unwilling either to ease Japanese failure, or to provide any quick or easy way to improve their hard lot. But the records since come to hand do not support the belief that a real chance of maintaining peace in the Pacific—on or close to the terms for which we had stood since 1931—was missed. They do not confirm the opinion that Konoye was prepared, without reserve or trickery, to observe the rules set down by Hull.[26] Nor that he would have been able to do so, even though a respite was granted and he was allowed to grade the retreat gently.

If Konoye was ready and able—as Grew thought—to give Roosevelt trustworthy and satisfactory promises of a new sort, he does not tell of them in his "Memoirs." Nor has any other record available to me disclosed them. He was a prisoner, willing or unwilling, of the terms precisely prescribed in conferences over

[26] For example, the decisions in regard to China. How reconcile two of Hull's principles (those stipulating non-intervention in domestic affairs and respect for the integrity and independence of China) with the terms specified on September 6 and reaffirmed by a Liaison Conference of September 13, as "Magic" revealed? China was to be required to assent to the stationing of Japanese Army units "for a necessary period" in prescribed areas in Inner Mongolia and North China, and for the stationing of Japanese warships and military units in Hainan, Amoy, and other localities. There was to be a Sino-Japanese economic coalition.

which he presided. The latest of these were the minimum demands specified by the Imperial Conference of September 6, just reviewed. It is unlikely that he could have got around them or that he would have in some desperate act discarded them. The whole of his political career speaks to the contrary.

In proof of his ability to carry out his assurances, Konoye stressed first, that his ideas were approved by the Army and Navy; and second, that senior officials (Vice-Chiefs of Staff) of both branches would accompany him on his mission. If and when he said "Yes," they would say "Yes"; and thus the United States could count upon unified execution of any accord. But it seems to me far more likely that the Army and Navy had other thoughts in mind on assigning high officials to go along with him. They would be there to see that Konoye did not yield to the wish for peace or the will of the President. The truer version of the bond is expressed in the title of one of the subsections of Konoye's "Memoirs": "The Independence of the Supreme Command and State Affairs from Each Other: The Anguish of Cabinets from Generation to Generation."

Konoye could have honestly agreed that Japan would stop its southern advance and reduce its forces in China to the minimum needed to assure compliance with its wishes. That is really all. To the seekers of the New Order in East Asia this seemed much; to the American government it seemed too little. The error, the fault, in American policy—if there was one—was not in the refusal to trust what Konoye could honestly offer. It was in insisting that Japan entirely clear out of Indo-China and China (and perhaps out of Manchukuo) and give up all exclusive privileges in these countries.

In any case, the President and Hull were convinced that Konoye's purposes were murky and his freedom of decision small. Therefore they concluded that to meet with him before Japan proved its intentions would be a great mistake.[27] It could bring confusion into both American policies and our relations with the other opponents of the Axis. So Grew's earnest appeal for a daring try did not influence the responses to Japan that Hull's drafting squad was putting together. They took nothing that came from Tokyo for granted; wanted everything shown. The Army and Navy were both saying that they could use well all the time they could get. Both Stimson and Knox approved "stringing out negotiations." But neither wanted Roosevelt to meet Konoye or to soften American terms just to gain time.[28]

Hull was guided by these thoughts in the prepared answer which he gave Nomura on October 2, the answer on which the plans of Japan hung. The Japanese proposals (of September 6), this said in effect, did not provide a basis for a settlement, and were on essential points ambiguous.[29] The meeting between the President and Konoye was put off till there was a real meeting of minds about the application of the four principles—which were the essential foundations of proper relations.

[27] Ott's judgment of the prospect was at the time the same as that reached by the American government. He thought that even though certain circles about Konoye genuinely sought a *détente* with the United States, the effort was certain to fail in the end. He reported that the purpose of Konoye's mission was being pictured to the Navy and activist circles as a last step to convince the Japanese people that a peaceful settlement was not possible. Acceptance of the American terms would, Ott predicted, swiftly result in grave inner convulsions. (See Most Urgent telegram, Ott to Ribbentrop, September 4, 1941. *Far East Mil. Trib.* Exh. No. 801A.)
[28] Stimson diary, entry for October 6, 1941.
[29] The text is to be found in *Foreign Relations: Japan*, II, 656, *et seq.*

Upon reading this, the opinion nurtured by Konoye and Toyoda, that Japanese and American terms could be reconciled, dropped. This, the note of October 2, rather than the one of November 26 on which controversy has centered, ended the era of talk. For the crisis that followed in Japan brought into power a group determined to fight us rather than move further our way. Thereafter war came first, diplomacy second. . . .

The American government, while talking with Japan, could not forget that it was allied with Germany and Italy. American planes and warships were now providing watch and ward over wide areas of the Middle and Western Atlantic and around Iceland.[30] Encounters were becoming frequent. On September 11 the President, having discussed his words with Hull, Stimson, and Knox, broadcast: "The aggression is not ours. Ours is solely defense. But let this warning be clear. From now on, if German or Italian vessels of war enter the waters, the protection of which is necessary for American defense, they do so at their own peril. The orders which I have given as Commander-in-Chief of the United States Army and Navy are to carry out that policy—at once."[31]

On September 26 the Navy issued orders to protect all ships engaged in commerce in our defensive waters—by patrolling, covering, escorting, reporting, or destroying German and Italian naval, land, and air forces encountered.[32] As the President wrote to Mackenzie King, Prime Minister of Canada, ". . . we have begun to have practically sole charge of the safety of things to twenty-six degrees longitude, and to a further extension in the waters well to the eastward of Iceland."[33]

Further, it was foreseen that before long American merchant ships, manned by American crews, would soon be making the whole voyage to Britain. By the end of September, agreement had been reached between the President and Congressional leaders that the Neutrality Act should be so amended as to permit American merchant ships to enter combat areas and the ports of belligerents. The President's message so recommending was sent to Congress October 8.

Would this bring war with Germany? Hull did not think so; Hitler would not, he thought, declare a war as a result of any action of ours unless he thought it to his own advantage.[34] But should this turn out to be wrong, how would Japan construe its obligations under Article III of the Tripartite Pact? It was not possible to deduce a reliable answer from either the Japanese talk or texts. The American government sought to have Japan, in

---

[30] On August 25 Atlantic fleet forces were ordered to destroy surface raiders which attacked shipping along sea lanes between North America and Iceland, or which approached these lanes sufficiently closely to threaten such shipping. On September 3 the Western Atlantic area of operations covered by the United States Atlantic fleet was extended eastward. These were changes, Nos. 2 and 4, to W.P.L. 51. *Pearl Harbor Attack*, Part 5, p. 2295.
[31] While this speech was in preparation, the President had the impulse to be more explicit in his statements but Hull warned against any reference to shooting.

[32] This was Western Hemisphere Defense Plan, No. 5 (W.P.L. 52), effective October 11, 1941.
[33] Letter, Roosevelt to King, September 27, 1941. Churchill understood these orders to mean that American ships would attack any Axis ships found in the prohibited zone and assume responsibility for all fast British convoys other than troop convoys between America and Iceland. See his message to General Smuts of September 14, 1941. Churchill, *The Grand Alliance*, p. 517.
[34] The event proved Hull to be correct. On September 17 the German Navy asked Hitler to change its orders to permit, among other things, attacks on escorting forces in any operational area at any time. Hitler decided against such action for the time being, until the outcome of the fighting in Russia was decided, which he expected soon. *Fuehrer Conferences*, 1941, II, 33.

some form or other, cancel the obligation. The Konoye Cabinet lived in an agony of division over the issue. Unwilling to separate from Germany, but equally unwilling to lose a chance for a settlement with the United States, it fell into bigamous vows. . . .

On November 5, the same day that the Japanese government decided to go to war if its final proposals (A or B) were rejected, Stark and Marshall (with Chiang Kai-shek's appeal before them) summed up their judgment of the line to be held. Their memorandum to the President advised that:

(a) The basic military policies and strategy agreed to in the United States-British Staff conversations remain sound. The primary objective of the two nations is the defeat of Germany. If Japan be defeated and Germany remain undefeated, decision will still have not been reached. In any case, an unlimited offensive war should not be undertaken against Japan, since such a war would greatly weaken the combined effort in the Atlantic against Germany, the most dangerous enemy.

(b) War between the United States and Japan should be avoided while building up defensive forces in the Far East, until such time as Japan attacks or directly threatens territories whose security to the United States is of very great importance. Military action against Japan should be undertaken only in one or more of the following contingencies: (1) A direct act of war by Japanese armed forces against the territory or mandated territory of the United States, the British Commonwealth, or the Netherlands East Indies; (2) The movement of Japanese armed forces into Thailand to the West of 100° East, or South of 10° North; or into Portuguese Timor, New Caledonia, or the Loyalty Islands.[35]

(d) Considering world strategy, a Japa-

nese advance against Kunming, into Thailand except as previously indicated, or an attack on Russia would not justify intervention by the United States against Japan.

(e) All possible aid short of actual war against Japan should be extended to the Chinese Central Government.

Specifically, they recommend:

That the dispatch of United States armed forces for intervention against Japan in China be disapproved.

That material aid to China be accelerated consonant with the needs of Russia, Great Britain, and our own forces.

That aid to the American Volunteer Group be continued and accelerated to the maximum practicable extent.

That no ultimatum be delivered to Japan.[36]

The President followed this traced line. On the 6th he told Stimson that he might propose a truce in which there would be no movement of armed forces for six months, during which China and Japan might come to terms. Stimson wanted time also but objected to this means of getting it. The movement of forces to the Philippines, he thought, should not be halted. And the Chinese, in his opinion, should not be left alone with the Japanese; they would, he correctly forecast, balk at any such arrangement.[37] The President placed the idea of a truce aside, but not far.

On this next day, November 7, the President asked the cabinet for advice. All agreed with a statement made by Hull that the situation was extremely serious and that Japan might attack at any time. The position being maintained in the talks with Japan was approved; the current program for the extension of military forces in the Southwest Pacific area was endorsed; the cohesion between our own activities in that area and those of Britain, Australia, and the Indies was noted with

[35] The thought was that any movement of this kind would be a plan to go into the Gulf of Siam, on the way to attack the Malay-Kra Peninsula.

[36] *Pearl Harbor Attack*, Part 14, pp. 1061–62.
[37] Stimson diary, entry for November 6, 1941.

satisfaction. Thus it was decided to "carry on," and to leave Japan to decide whether to turn about or attack. The President took a poll, asking whether the people would back the government up if it struck at Japan in case it attacked English or Dutch territories in the Pacific. All the cabinet was of the opinion that it would. It was agreed that speeches should be made to acquaint the country with the situation.[38]

In the evening after this cabinet meeting Nomura paid his first call on Hull since the advent of the Tojo Cabinet. Earnestly he presented Proposal A and asked a quick answer. Hull, after a rapid glance at the contents (which he already knew) indicated his attitude by observing what a wonderful chance Japan had to launch forth on a real new order which would gain it moral leadership in the Far East.

Nomura asked to talk to the President, and was received on the 10th. He had an invisible naval escort not of his own choosing. Not many hours before he entered the White House, his former colleague, Vice-Admiral Nagumo, on board the aircraft carrier *Akagi,* issued Striking Force Operations Order, No. 1. All ships in this force were directed to complete battle preparations by November 20, and to assemble in Hitokappu Bay, Etorofu Island, Kuriles. This was the force that was to attack Pearl Harbor.

Nomura did not know either the schedule or geography written in this order, one of many placing the Japanese Navy in location for war. But he knew that he was in a race with such orders, and that only some miracle of conversion could stop them. The smoke was over the funnels. Thus he pleaded for acceptance of

what he came to offer on the ground that Japan was doing all it could in the light of reason and of history. But his two American listeners were unmoved. Their books, open and secret, contained the record of Japan's desertion of the ways of peace and order. . . .

Nomura placed Proposal B before Hull on November 20. The English text, as cabled some days before, had been intercepted and read. Hull knew that it was regarded in Tokyo as the last bargain; the hinge on the breech of the cannon.

There were five numbered points on the white piece of paper which Nomura gave to Hull. They have been printed in many other places, but I think the reader will want them before him as he follows the narrative:

1. Both the Government of Japan and the United States undertake not to make any armed advancement into any of the regions in the South-eastern Asia and the Southern Pacific area excepting the part of French Indo-China where the Japanese troops are stationed at present.

2. The Japanese Government undertakes to withdraw its troops now stationed in French Indo-China upon either the restoration of peace between Japan and China or the establishment of an equitable peace in the Pacific area.

In the meantime the Government of Japan declares that it is prepared to remove its troops now stationed in the southern part of French Indo-China to the northern part of the said territory upon the conclusion of the present arrangement which shall later be embodied in the final agreement.

3. The Government of Japan and the United States shall cooperate with a view to securing the acquisition of those goods and commodities which the two countries need in Netherlands East Indies.

4. The Government of Japan and the United States mutually undertake to restore their commercial relations to those prevailing prior to the freezing of the assets.

[38] *Ibid.,* entry for November 7, and the written statement by Hull, *Pearl Harbor Attack,* Part 2, p. 429.

The Government of the United States shall supply Japan a required quantity of oil.

5. The Government of the United States undertakes to refrain from such measures and actions as will be prejudiced to the endeavors for the restoration of general peace between Japan and China."[39]

Whoever insisted on the last paragraph —Tojo and the Army certainly did—insisted on war.

Hull glanced over the text to make sure it was the same as that which was known. It was. Then, on two points in particular, he spoke out. Linking Japan's treatment of China to Hitler's actions, he defended our aid to China. Kurusu remarked that perhaps this point (No. 5) in the Japanese terms might be construed to mean that the United States would end its help only at the time when talks between Japan and China would have started. Hull also dwelt on the fact that this truce would leave Japan a full member of the Axis pact, and hence still a potential enemy of the United States and Great Britain. To this Kurusu had no answer.[40]

Hull found no dissent, either within the State Department or at the White House, to his opinion that the proposal was "clearly unacceptable." His reasons for finding it so are summed up again in his "Memoirs":

The commitments we should have to make were virtually a surrender. We on our part should have to supply Japan as much oil as she might require, suspend our freezing measures, and resume full commercial relations with Tokyo. We should have to discontinue aid to China and withdraw our moral and material support from the recognized Chinese Government of Chiang Kai-shek. We should have to help Japan obtain products of the Netherlands East Indies. We should have to cease augmenting our military forces in the western Pacific.

Japan, on her part, would still be free to continue her military operations in China, to attack the Soviet Union, and to keep her troops in northern Indo-China until peace was effected with China. . . . Japan thus clung to her vantage point in Indo-China which threatened countries to the south and vital trade routes.

The President and I could only conclude that agreeing to these proposals would mean condonement by the United States of Japan's past aggressions, assent to future courses of conquest by Japan, abandonment of the most essential principles of our foreign policy, betrayal of China and Russia, and acceptance of the role of silent partner aiding and abetting Japan in her effort to create a Japanese hegemony over the western Pacific and eastern Asia.[41]

* * *

War might be in the secret messages; it might be in the nerves; but the wish to avoid it was still alive. Hull began to compound a counter-offer to Proposal B which might defer the climax without giving Japan an advantage, or destroying the faith of our allies. The drafting squad ransacked the files for old memoranda, and drew upon a refreshingly new one from the Treasury. . . .

The very making of the offer seemed likely to have troublesome, if not ruinous, effects. It would be self-defeating to give a true and full explanation to the American people. A confused domestic debate was apt to follow and be in full flow when the war crisis came. More worrisome still was the prospect that, despite whatever was said, the other nations fighting the Axis would feel let down. There was no time to convince Chiang Kai-shek that China would not suffer and would not be deserted.[42] The other members of the

[39] *Foreign Relations: Japan,* II, 755–56.
[40] *Ibid.,* II, 753–55.

[41] Hull, *op. cit.,* II, 1069–70.
[42] The intercepted message, No. 821, from Togo to Nomura on the 24th read in part: ". . . our demand for a cessation of aid to Chiang . . . is a most essential condition." *Loc. cit.*

coalition were showing themselves luke-warm—not opposing the truce, but not welcoming it. Was it, as Hull averred, only a maneuver, or was it a wavering in the ranks?

Sometime during the night of the 25th, Churchill's answer to the President arrived.[43] It left the American government free to do what it thought best, but seemed to fall in with the view that a truce with Japan was unfair to China. Doubt seemed to overrule enthusiasm. The text is given so that the reader may judge for himself:[44]

Most Secret for the President from the Former Naval Person. "Your message about Japan received tonight. Also full accounts from Lord Halifax of discussions and your counter project to Japan on which Foreign Secretary has sent some comments. Of course, it is for you to han-dle this business and we certainly do not want an additional war. There is only one point that disquiets us. What about Chiang Kai-shek? Is he not having a very thin diet? Our anxiety is about China. If they collapse our joint dangers would enormously increase. We are sure that the regard of the United States for the Chinese cause will govern your action. We feel that the Japanese are most unsure of themselves."[45]

Hull, in the course of the night, added up the sum of pros and cons. The reason for going ahead with the counterproposal had come to seem unreal. What we had to offer, it was all but certain, would not buy even time. The objections seemed many and hard to meet. He decided to discard it and let events take their course. The verdict was reached after tormenting uncertainty. But once reached, a calm sense followed that he had done all that a man could do. . . .

The long Ten-Point Memorandum on principles, which was our response to Proposal B, was received in Tokyo on the morning of the 27th. Along with it Nomura and Kurusu sent a convoy of troubled comment. They thought the answer hard and dumbfounding. But they found nothing in it compelling Japan to resort to war. They were afraid, as "Magic" let Washington know, that the United States and Britain might try to forestall Japan by occupying the Indies, thus bringing on war. Even this late, Nomura advised his government to keep on with the effort to reach a peaceful accord. He recalled a remark the President had made in an earlier talk—that there would be "no last words."[46] But, he added, if his counsel was not taken, it would be best not to keep up a false front of friendliness, and

---

[43] There is a conflict of report as to when this cable or its substance was known to the President and Hull. According to the time stamps on the face of the original, it was sent from London at 6 A.M. on November 26, received by the code room of the State Department at 12:55 A.M., November 26, which is before the time of dispatch, allowance being made for five hours' time difference. It also carries the notation that it was sent over to the White House at 9:05 A.M. on the 26th.

But two of the participants in the afternoon and evening meetings with Hull on the 25th have the remembered impression that either the cable or the substance of it was known to them then; they recall even Hull's comments that Churchill's message did not seem to agree entirely with Eden's. Despite the absence of any record, it is possible that the substance of this message was transmitted earlier in the day through the British Embassy in Washington or some other channel. Hull's reference to this point in his book (*op. cit.*, II, 1081) can be read either way, but suggests that Hull knew its contents on the night of the 25th.

[44] In the minute that Churchill sent to Eden on November 23 he indicated favor towards the counterproposal being prepared by the State Department, provided the United States and Britain remained free to continue their aid to China. But on this point he found the draft which Hull submitted inadequate. Churchill, *The Grand Alliance*, pp. 595–96.

[45] *Pearl Harbor Attack*, Part 14, p. 1300.
[46] Intercepted Telegrams, Nos. 1180, 1189, and 1190, Nomura to Togo, November 26, 1941, set forth the Ambassador's views at length.

to strike from behind it. Kurusu, also, tried to be calming. He attributed our statement in part to knowledge of the Japanese military movements and concentrations in the south.[47]

Another Liaison Conference was called as soon as the American paper was read (November 27). This summarily dismissed our statement of principles as a humiliating ultimatum. It was resolved to proceed with the program adopted on November 5; that is, to go to war as soon as the striking forces were in position. Stratagem had failed. Force would be used. Japan would do or die.

As was natural, the men who made this decision pleaded later that it was compelled by the terms placed upon peace by the United States. Thus, the former Foreign Minister, Togo, one of the more conciliatory members of the government, argued that "Japan was now asked not only to abandon all the gains of her years of sacrifice, but to surrender her international position as a power in the Far East. That surrender, as he saw it, would have amounted to national suicide. The only way to face this challenge and defend ourselves was war."[48]

This was not a valid attitude. The idea that compliance with the American terms would have meant "extinction" for Japan, or so deeply hurt it that it could not guard its just interests, is an absurdity. Japan was not asked to give up any land or resources except those which it held by force of arms. Its independence was not in peril. Its Army, Navy, and Air Force would have remained in being. Its chances to trade with the rest of the world would have been restored. Its struggle against the extension of communism could have combined with that of China and the West. Extinction threatened the plan for expansion in Asia, but not Japan or the Japanese.

[47] Telegram, No. 1206, Nomura to Togo, November 27, and memorandum of telephone conversation between Kurusu and Yamamoto on November 27.

[48] Togo deposition, *Far East Mil. Trib.*, Exh. No. 3646.

Charles A. Beard: APPEARANCES AND REALITIES

The late Charles A. Beard, one of the most eminent historians of his generation and a past president of the American Historical Association, is well-known for his criticisms of United States foreign policy. In American Foreign Policy in the Making, 1932-1940 *and* President Roosevelt and the Coming of the War, 1941, *from which the present selection is taken, Beard contends that the Administration rejected sincere proposals for peace and deceived the American people. Though maintaining that his policy was to stay out of war, Roosevelt, Beard believes, purposely followed a policy that embroiled us in war.*

Secret War Decisions and Plans

THERE is also now available sufficient evidence respecting two primary questions with which my inquiry is particularly concerned: (1) How did the secret actions of the Roosevelt Administration bearing on relations with Japan from August 17 to December 7, 1941, as described in official documents now available, square with official representations of the Administration to the American people at the time—realities with appearances? (2) Do these official documents sustain the official thesis respecting relations with Japan presented to Congress and the people by President Roosevelt's message to Congress on December 8, 1941?

On that occasion, the President said—to repeat, for convenience—that on December 7, 1941, the United States was at peace with Japan, that at the solicitation of Japan it was still in conversation with the Japanese Government and Emperor, looking toward the maintenance of peace in the Pacific, and that on that day Japan had undertaken a planned "surprise offensive," of which the attack on Pearl Harbor was a phase. Did the course of American-Japanese affairs as conducted during the months preceding Pearl Harbor, however it "looked," actually point in the direction of peace with Japan? Were those affairs in such a state at any time during this period that the President actually expected them to eventuate in the maintenance of peace in the Pacific? Did the Japanese Government make any proposals during this period which looked to the possibility of maintaining peace in the Pacific? And, if so, how did Secretary Hull and President Roosevelt treat these proposals with a view to the maintenance of peace? Did the President think that the Japanese final memorandum delivered to Secretary Hull on December 7 actually constituted no threat or hint of an armed attack? Was the Japanese offensive really a surprise to the Administration? With reference to these questions there are some answers in the documents now available.

As early as October 8, 1940, during the campaign of that year while he was still making peace pledges to the country, President Roosevelt had become convinced that Japan would make a mistake and that the United States would enter a war in the Pacific. He expressed this conviction to Admiral J. O. Richardson,

From *President Roosevelt and the Coming of the War, 1941* by Charles A. Beard (New Haven: Yale University Press, 1948), excerpted material from pages 484–516. Reprinted by permission.

Commander in Chief of the Fleet in the Pacific, whose duty it was to prepare plans for the war thus foretold by the President.[1] The development of an American war plan, based on arrangements made with the British Commonwealth and the Netherlands in the spring of 1941, contemplated a general war in which the United States would participate when and if it came[2]—a plan which President Roosevelt approved, "except officially," to use Admiral Stark's ingenious phrase.

On December 14, 1940, the American Ambassador in Tokyo, Joseph Grew, wrote a long letter to President Roosevelt on American-Japanese relations, in the course of which he said that, unless the United States was prepared to withdraw bag and baggage from the entire sphere of Greater East Asia and the South Seas, "(which God forbid), we are bound eventually to come to a head-on clash with Japan." President Roosevelt replied, January 21, 1941, "I find myself in decided agreement with your conclusions"; and went on to say that "our strategy of self-defense must be a global strategy which takes account of every front and takes advantage of every opportunity to contribute to our total security."[3] In other words, in January 1941, President Roosevelt envisaged a head-on clash with Japan as a phase of assistance to Great Britain in a world of inseparable spheres of interest. This conclusion squared with the conviction he had expressed to Admiral Richardson on October 8, 1940: Japan will make a mistake and we will enter the war....

President Roosevelt's Warning Note to Japan on August 17, 1941

On August 17, 1941, after his return from the Atlantic Conference, President Roosevelt called the Japanese Ambassador to the White House and told him point-blank, among other things:

... this Government now finds it necessary to say to the Government of Japan that if the Japanese Government takes any further steps in pursuance of a policy or program of military domination by force or threat of force of neighboring countries, the Government of the United States will be compelled to take immediately any and all steps which it may deem necessary toward safeguarding the legitimate rights and interests of the United States and American nationals and toward insuring the safety and security of the United States.

Such was the formula of the President's warning as recorded in the State Department's *Peace and War,* published in July, 1943 (p. 714).[4]

To the Japanese Ambassador, familiar with the language of diplomacy, the statement could have had only one meaning. Although the President did not even hint

---

[1] See above, p. 416.

[2] See above, pp. 442 ff.

[3] Joseph C. Grew, *Ten Years in Japan* (Simon & Schuster, 1944), pp. 359 ff.

[4] I searched the files of the *New York Times* and the *New York Herald Tribune* from August 17 to August 31, 1941, for references to press releases or statements from the White House and the State Department bearing on the delivery of this warning notice to Ambassador Nomura and found no such reference. Later I had two independent searches made of these files by two scholars trained in historical research and neither of them found even a hint that this note had been delivered to the Japanese Ambassador. On December 16, 1946, I wrote to the State Department asking whether the department had issued any statement or press release on the note of August 17, 1941, and received a reply dated January 3, 1947, which did not constitute an answer. In a letter dated January 7, 1947, I directed this question to the State Department: "Did the Department of State issue on or after August 17, 1941, any press release or statement to the press notifying the public that the important memorandum of August 17, 1941, had been delivered to the Japanese Ambassador in Washington on that day?" In a letter dated January 21, 1947, the State Department said: "the records of the Department indicate that a press release was not issued on the subject to which you refer."

that he would appeal to Congress for a declaration of war if the Japanese Government failed to heed his warning, he did indicate that if that government took any further steps in the direction of dominating neighboring countries, by force or threat of force, the United States would do something besides send another diplomatic memorandum to Tokyo. . . .

In the memoranda made by Mr. Welles on the meetings at the Atlantic Conference it is patent that the notice given by President Roosevelt to the Japanese Ambassador on August 17, 1941, was intended to be in the nature of a war warning. It is true that in the final form given to the notice, two points brought up at the Atlantic Conference had been eliminated or softened. Mr. Churchill's suggestion that the President inform Japan that he intended to seek authority from Congress to implement his notice was rejected. Also eliminated from the draft dated August 15, 1941, were the words: "notwithstanding the possibility that such further steps on its [Japan's] part may result in conflict between the two countries"; for these words were substituted a formula more veiled, but scarcely any less meaningful to Ambassador Nomura and the Government of Japan.

The Japanese Government's Proposal for a Pacific Conference Rejected

Numerous "leaks" in Washington, noncommittal releases from the Department of State, and rumors kept the American public in expectancy—and confusion. In fact, at one time, when it was openly said in newspaper circles that arrangements had been made for a meeting of President Roosevelt and Premier Konoye, this "rumor" was brushed aside humorously by the President's Secretary, Stephen Early, at the White House.[5]

[5] See above, p. 189.

Although, during the tortuous exchanges of notes on the proposed conference in the Pacific, the American public remained in the dark with regard to the nature of the various offers and counteroffers, documents made available since December 7, 1941, have partly disclosed the nature of the tactics employed by President Roosevelt and Secretary Hull in conducting those exchanges. . . .

The strategy pursued by the President and the Secretary of State during these conversations on the Japanese Premier's proposal for a peace conference in the Pacific was, in brief, as follows. The President and the Secretary expressed to Japan a willingness to consider favorably the idea of a Pacific Conference, but insisted that the Premier should first agree upon certain principles in advance, with a view to assuring the success of the conference.

The Premier of Japan, on September 6, 1941, informed the American ambassador in Tokyo that he subscribed fully to the four great principles of American policy laid down in Washington.[6] Then President Roosevelt and Secretary Hull declared that this was not enough, that agreements on more principles and formulas was necessary, that the replies of the Japanese Government were still unsatisfactory; but they refrained from saying in precise language just what it was they demanded in detail as fixed conditions for accepting the Japanese invitation to a conference in the Pacific. To meet their obvious distrust of Japanese authorities and especially the Japanese militarists, Premier Konoye assured them that he had authority for bringing with him to the conference high army and naval officers as evidence that his commitments would have the support of the Army and the Navy of Japan. Still the

[6] *Peace and War*, pp. 733 ff.

51

President and the Secretary continued adamant in their tactics of prolonging the conversations as if they were merely playing for time, "babying the Japanese along."

It may be said that President Roosevelt and Secretary Hull thus chose a course well within their discretion, and demonstrated wisdom in so doing. That militarists in the Japanese Government and outside had been engaged in barbaric practices in China for many years and were rattling the sabers in the autumn of 1941 was a matter of general knowledge in the United States. That the Roosevelt Administration had long been opposed to Japan's policies and measures was, at least, equally well known. Still, if keeping out of war in the Pacific was a serious issue for the United States, then the primary question for President Roosevelt and Secretary Hull was: Did the Japanese proposal offer an opportunity to effect a settlement in the Pacific and were the decisions they made in relation to it actually "looking" in the direction of peace?...

Aware that in negotiations with the Japanese Ambassador in Washington, President Roosevelt and Secretary Hull were insisting upon further explorations of the Japanese proposal and that more than a month had passed in these "exploratory" operations, Mr. Grew warned them against this procedure. He told them that if the United States expected or awaited "clear-cut commitments" which would satisfy the United States "both as to principle and as to concrete detail," the conversations would be drawn out indefinitely and unproductively "until the Konoye cabinet and its supporting elements desiring rapprochement with the United States will come to the conclusion that the outlook for an agreement is hopeless and that the United States

Government is only playing for time."[7] In this case, the Ambassador continued, the Konoye Government would be discredited. "The logical outcome of this will be the downfall of the Konoye cabinet and the formation of a military dictatorship which will lack either the disposition or the temperament to avoid colliding head-on with the United States."

If Premier Konoye was sincere in his intentions why could he not give President Roosevelt and Secretary Hull clear-cut commitments as to details before the conference? To this central question Ambassador Grew gave serious attention and provided for the President and the Secretary an answer based on his knowledge of the critical situation in Tokyo. Mr. Grew knew that a "liberal" government in Japan, or indeed any government inclined to keep peace with the United States, was beset by the militarist and chauvinist press, always engaged in frightening and inflaming the Japanese public by warmongering. He knew also, what had recently been demonstrated many times, that the head and members of any such government were likely to be assassinated in cold blood by desperate agents of "patriotic" societies. He knew and so did Premier Konoye that Axis secret agents and Japanese enemies of peace with the United States were boring within the Konoye Government and watching with Argus eyes every message or communication sent from Tokyo to Washington. In other words, Premier Konoye could not be sure that any note he dispatched to Washington, no matter how guardedly, would escape the vigilance of his enemies on every side in Japan.

[7] Did this mean that the Japanese would suspect that President Roosevelt's intention was "to baby them along," as Davis and Lindley represented his designs at the Atlantic Conference? *How War Came*, p. 10.

This situation Ambassador Grew went into at length in his report of September 29, 1941, to Secretary Hull and President Roosevelt. He had been in close and confidential communication with Premier Konoye. On the basis of very intimate knowledge, he informed them that the Japanese Government was ready to undertake commitments other than those set down in the communications which had already passed. He reported, if in cautious language as befitted a diplomat, that he had been told that "Prince Konoye is in a position in direct negotiations with President Roosevelt to offer him assurances which, because of their far-reaching character, will not fail to satisfy the United States." Mr. Grew added that he could not determine the truth of this statement, but he said definitely that while the Japanese Government could not overtly renounce its relations with the Axis Powers, it "actually has shown a readiness to reduce Japan's alliance adherence to a dead letter by its indication of willingness to enter formally into negotiations with the United States."

Thereupon Mr. Grew presented the alternatives as he saw them from his point of vantage in Tokyo. The Japanese military machine and army could be discredited by wholesale military defeat. That was one alternative. On the other hand the United States could place a "reasonable amount of confidence" in

the professed sincerity of intention and good faith of Prince Konoye and his supporters to mold Japan's future policy upon the basic principles they are ready to accept and then to adopt measures which gradually but loyally implement those principles, with it understood that the United States will implement its own commitments *pari passu* with the steps which Japan takes.

This was the alternative which the American Ambassador commended to President Roosevelt and Secretary Hull as "an attempt to produce a regeneration of Japanese thought and outlook through constructive conciliation, along the lines of American efforts at present."

As to the alternatives, Mr. Grew closed his plea by inquiring "whether the better part of wisdom and of statesmanship is not to bring such efforts to a head before the force of their initial impetus is lost, leaving it impossible to overcome an opposition which the Ambassador thinks will mount inevitably and steadily in Japan." In Mr. Grew's opinion it was evidently a question of now or never, though he ended by paying deference to "the much broader field of view of President Roosevelt and Secretary Hull" as compared with "the viewpoint of the American Embassy in Tokyo." ...

Nevertheless, President Roosevelt and Secretary Hull rejected the advice of their Ambassador in Japan and prolonged the "explorations" until the Konoye Cabinet fell about two weeks later, October 16, 1941. Why? Records now available provide no answer. As far as the President was concerned, the question remains open, save for such inferences as may be drawn from collateral documents. Secretary Hull's answer is to be sought in many words spread over many pages, and, owing to the fact that he was the President's agent in the conduct of foreign affairs, his answer, by inference, may be treated as that of the Administration. When Secretary Hull's prolix and involved explanations as yet presented to the American public are all analyzed, compared, and tabulated, they amount to this: The Japanese had a long record of barbaric deeds: Prince Konoye was not much better, if any, than the bloodthirsty militarists; the promises and proposals of the Konoye Government were not to be trusted as offering any hope of peace to the "peace-loving nations of the world," as represented by the United States. ...

In other words, the President and Secretary Hull regarded the Japanese proposal for a Pacific Conference as essentially dishonest, as if a kind of subterfuge to deceive the Government of the United States while Japan went on with aggression and conquest.

It is at present impossible to determine the parts played by President Roosevelt and Secretary Hull respectively in the final decision to reject the Konoye proposal, as it is in the case of their action on the memorandum of November 26, 1941. According to Premier Konoye's Memoirs (CJC, Part 20, Exhibit 173), the President was at first enthusiastic about the idea of a conference in the Pacific but Secretary Hull was at the outset cool and at length resolute in pursuing the course which, as Ambassador Grew had warned him in effect, would end in failure and war.

Nor is it possible now to discover whether, if the Pacific conference had been held, Premier Konoye could have carried out his intentions as communicated to the President and Secretary Hull. It is easy, of course, to take passages from Premier Konoye's Memoirs, and other fragmentary documents at present available, for the purpose of making an argument for or against American acceptance of his proposal; but, as Ambassador Grew informed the President and Secretary Hull at the time, the alternative of war would remain open to the United States if the conference had not fulfilled expectations. The "solution" of this insoluble "problem," however, lies outside the purposes and limitations of my inquiry.

The Japanese Proposal of a Modus Vivendi Rejected in Favor of an Ultimative Notice

Though the Konoye Cabinet in Tokyo had been succeeded by what we regarded as a "strong" government headed by General Hideki Tojo, supposed to be an irreconcilable militarist, the Japanese did not break off conversations "looking to the maintenance of peace in the Pacific." On the contrary, the Japanese Government early in November dispatched to Ambassador Nomura two proposals for new discussions to be taken up with President Roosevelt and Secretary Hull and sent a special agent, Saburo Kurusu, to assist the Ambassador in further explorations. The first of these proposals, called proposal "A," was plainly a document for bargaining; the second, proposal "B," was more conciliatory and had the signs of being the last offer the Japanese Government might make to the United States— "a last effort to prevent something happening." Was this move on the part of Japan just another evidence of what Secretary Hull called Japanese trickery, a desire to prolong negotiations and to deceive the Government of the United States?

On their face the two proposals, as finally presented to the State Department, might have been so regarded by Secretary Hull. But as a matter of fact, having previously broken the Japanese code, American Navy and Army Intelligence had intercepted, translated, and made available to the Administration, before either of the projects had been laid before Secretary Hull, the substance of the two documents as sent in code from Tokyo to Ambassador Nomura. It had done more. It had intercepted accompanying messages from Tokyo to the Ambassador which indicated, in the first place, that the Tojo Cabinet was anxious to reach some kind of settlement with the United States; and, in the next place, that the second proposal was, to use the language of the Japanese dispatch containing it, "advanced with the idea of making a last effort to prevent something from happening." If the opinion often expressed by

Secretary Hull to the effect that the Japanese were chronic liars be accepted as correct, still it is hardly to be presumed that the Japanese Government was lying to its Ambassador when, in secret messages intended for his eyes alone, it informed him that a settlement was urgently desired in Tokyo and that proposal "B" was to be offered in a last effort to prevent something from happening— that is, doubtless, an open break and war.[8]

In short, Secretary Hull knew in advance, on November 4, 1941, that the Japanese proposals were coming to him, that the Tokyo Government had expressed to Ambassador Nomura anxiety to reach some settlement with the United States, that it had fixed November 25 as a deadline, that failure to achieve a settlement or truce meant drastic action, if not war, on the part of the Japanese Government. On November 1, Secretary Hull had asked the Army and Navy whether they were ready to give support to new warnings to Japan, and expressed the opinion that there was no use to issue any additional warnings "if we can't back them up."[9] On November 5, General Marshall and Admiral Stark addressed to

President Roosevelt a memorandum in which they strongly objected to military action against Japan at the moment and urged the postponement of hostilities in order to allow the Army and Navy as much time as possible to effect better preparations for war.[10] It was in this state of affairs that Secretary Hull undertook to deal with Ambassador Nomura when he presented a sketch of proposal "A," November 7, 1941. . . .

When President Roosevelt and Secretary Hull were called upon to make decisions with regard to the Japanese program for a kind of modus vivendi looking to a general settlement in the Pacific, they confronted a fateful choice and they knew it. From secret Japanese messages intercepted by the Army and Navy Intelligence, they had learned that this proposal was the final offering from the Japanese Government. They confronted the urgent appeal from General Marshall and Admiral Stark to postpone hostilities with Japan on the ground that the Army and Navy were not ready for war. Should at least a truce of some form be attempted if only to give the United States more time to prepare for war? The idea of a truce had been taken up by the President with Secretary Stimson as early as November 6, two days after the secret Japanese message on the negotiations had been intercepted.[11] And Mr. Stimson had strongly objected to the idea.[12]

Despite Secretary Stimson's objections, however, the President apparently decided that a truce or modus vivendi might and should be attempted; for he sent an undated note to Secretary Hull, giving his suggestions for the terms of such a tem-

---

[8] CJC, Part 12, Exhibit 1, for the two proposals, pp. 94–97; for various relevant Japanese messages, intercepted and translated by American Intelligence, pp. 90 ff.

[9] At a meeting of the Joint Board of the Army and Navy, November 3, 1941, General Marshall and Admiral Stark present, among others, Captain R. E. Schuirmann, liaison officer between the Office of Naval Operations and the State Department, reported on actions at the State Department meeting on November 1. Captain Schuirmann "pointed out that on August 17, following the President's return from the meeting at sea with Mr. Churchill, the President had issued an ultimatum to Japan that it would be necessary for the United States to take action in case of further Japanese aggression. . . . Mr. Hull was of the opinion that there was no use to issue any additional warnings to Japan if we can't back them up, and he desired to know if the military authorities would be prepared to support further warnings by the State Department." CJC, Part 14, p. 1063. The Japanese

deadline was later moved to November 29. CJC, Part 20, p. 165.
[10] CJC, Part 12, Exhibit 1; Part 14, Exhibits 16, 18.
[11] See above, pp. 507 ff.
[12] Stimson, *Diary*, for November 6, 1941.

porary or preliminary adjustment with Japan. The President's note contained the following points:

6 Months

1. United States to resume economic relations—some oil and rice now—more later.
2. Japan to send no more troops to Indo-China or Manchurian border or any place South (Dutch, Brit. or Siam).
3. Japan to agree not to invoke tripartite pact even if the U.S. gets into European war.
4. U.S. to introduce Japs to Chinese to talk things over but U.S. to take no part in their conversation. . . .

* * *

Alarmed lest the Government of the United States make something like a truce or temporary standstill with Japan, with a view to further negotiation actually looking to the maintenance of peace in the Pacific, Chinese diplomatic and special agents, supported by powerful American interests, made a storm over the proposed modus vivendi with Japan. In this operation, they were ably led by the Chinese Ambassador, Dr. Hu Shih, a liberal, wise in the ways of the West and the East, once well marked by the dread police of the Chiang Kai-shek Government, now serving it in the United States where "liberalism" was an asset. From day to day, hour to hour, the Chinese and their agents bombarded Secretary Hull so heavily with protests against any truce with Japan that the situation in Washington became almost hysterical.

This state of affairs was later described by Secretary Hull himself. The Secretary, in a subsequent statement relative to the pressures then brought to bear on him by the Chinese, declared that Chiang Kai-shek "has sent numerous hysterical cable messages to different cabinet officers and high officials in the Government other than the State Department, and some-

times even ignoring the President, intruding into a delicate and serious situation with no real idea of what the facts are." Secretary Hull further said that "Chiang Kai-shek had his brother-in-law, located here in Washington, disseminate damaging reports at times to the press and others, apparently with no particular purpose in mind." Besieged by Chinese agents in London, Prime Minister Churchill, instead of supporting his Ambassador in Washington, Lord Halifax, who was eager for a truce in the Pacific, intervened by sending a confusing message as if trying to support the Chinese side of the dispute with the Government of the United States.

Disturbed by the vacillations introduced by Mr. Churchill's intrusion into American affairs, Secretary Hull exclaimed that

it would have been better if, when Churchill received Chiang Kai-shek's loud protest about our negotiations here with Japan, instead of passing the protest on to us without objection on his part, thereby qualifying and virtually killing what we knew were the individual views of the British Government toward these negotiations, he had sent a strong cable back to Chiang Kai-shek telling him to brace up and fight with the same zeal as the Japanese and the Germans are displaying instead of weakening and telling the Chinese people that all of the friendly countries were now striving primarily to protect themselves and to force an agreement between China and Japan. Every Chinese should understand from such a procedure that the best possible course was being pursued and that this calls for resolute fighting until the undertaking is consummated by peace negotiations which Japan in due course would be obliged to enter into with China.[13]

In other words, while the negotiations over the Japanese proposal for a modus

[13] CJC, Part 14, pp. 1194 ff.

vivendi were proceeding, Secretary Hull was disgusted with the operations of Chinese agents. He was convinced that the tentatives of the proposal should be explored and efforts be made to reach some kind of basis for further explorations in the direction of a settlement in the Far East. He was likewise convinced that in the proceedings along this line the real interests of China could be protected by the United States, indeed advanced, until, at least, the willingness of Japan to come to decent terms could be probed to the bottom. So at least, it seems.

But for reasons which are nowhere explicit, despite the thousands of words on the subject that appear in the Pearl Harbor documents and testimony, Secretary Hull, after consulting President Roosevelt, suddenly and completely abandoned the project and on November 26, 1941, handed the Japanese Ambassador and Mr. Kurusu the historic memorandum which the Japanese Government treated as an ultimatum.[14] When the Japanese

[14] For the nature and significance of this memo-

representatives in Washington read the document, Mr. Kurusu assured the Secretary that the Japanese Government, after examining it, would be likely to throw up its hands. When, the next morning, Secretary Stimson asked Secretary Hull what had been done about the modus vivendi project, the Secretary replied that "he had broken the whole matter off." He then added: "I have washed my hands of it and it is now in the hands of you and Knox—the Army and the Navy. . . ."[15]

randum, see above, Chap. IX; and for the upshot of the decision to send it, see below, pp. 555 ff.

[15] Alden Hatch, who claims to have inside information from prominent persons close to President Roosevelt at the time, seems to ascribe this momentous decision mainly to Secretary Hull, for he says: "Roosevelt was uncertain if he had done the right thing in allowing Hull to present his ten-point program to Japan on November 26. Though it offered them great economic concessions, and the access to the goods of the Indies that they desired, it called on them to desist in China. He feared they would never do that." *Franklin D. Roosevelt: An Informal Biography*, p. 289.

Basil Rauch: PRINCIPLE IN INTERNATIONAL POLICY

In the book from which the following selection is secured Professor Basil Rauch, diplomatic historian at Barnard College and Columbia University, takes direct issue with Charles A. Beard, point by point criticizing the latter's use of the evidence and reaching quite opposite conclusions. Rauch represents the point of view which emphasizes the importance of principles of morality and international law in determining policies that the United States could embrace.

Introduction

DURING the decade 1933–1942, world events and President Franklin D. Roosevelt led the American people and their government to adopt collective security as the foreign policy of the United States. The late Dr. Charles A. Beard is the only historian who has written on the process by which the nation abandoned isolationism and turned to internationalism. His two books, *American Foreign Policy in the Making: 1932–1940: A Study in Responsibilities,* and *President Roosevelt and the Coming of the War: 1941: A Study in Appearances and Realities,* frankly aim to destroy the faith of Americans in the honesty of President Roosevelt in planning the new foreign policy.

These books propose a revisionist interpretation of the causes of American entry into the Second World War. After the First World War, revisionist historians won over the American public to their view that the United States had entered that war not because Germany committed aggression against it, but because American bankers and munitions manufacturers plotted entry for their own profit. The thesis provided justification for the return to isolationism. Beard's purpose was to create a similar disillusionment regarding the reasons for American entry into the recent war, and a similar revulsion against the foreign policy of internationalism.

The villain in Beard's plot is not an economic group with a vested interest in war, but the President of the United States acting for motives which are not defined. The picture of President Roosevelt engaged in a colossal and profoundly immoral plot to deceive the American people into participating in the war unnecessarily and contrary to their interests might be thought so overdrawn as to be unconvincing. But Beard relies upon the effects of the twelve and more years of widely publicized hatred of Roosevelt by a minority of the public and the majority of the press to make the familiarity of his characterization overcome its implausibility.

An indication of Beard's desire to capitalize on anti-Roosevelt feeling is that in his two books he almost completely ignores the part Secretary of State Hull played in the making of administration foreign policy. Hull's work was certainly second in importance only to that of the President himself, and in details it was

Reprinted from *Roosevelt: From Munich to Pearl Harbor* by Basil Rauch, by permission of Farrar and Straus & Company, Inc. Copyright © 1950 by Basil Rauch. From pages 1–2, 445, 446–47, & 467–477.

more revealing than Roosevelt's. But, because Hull was generally regarded as an honest and safe leader, his presence on Beard's stage as Roosevelt's partner would have been an inartistic contradiction of Beard's image of Roosevelt pursuing a sinister plot.

This is only one of the many artful exclusions Beard practices. More important is his exclusion of any data on the objective course of world events which might suggest that the United States, confronted by rising Axis power, did actually face danger to its own security. In Beard's books, not policies of Hitler or Japan but the policies of Roosevelt created first the danger and then the fact of United States participation in the Second World War. In the early pages of *American Foreign Policy in the Making*, Beard shows admirable, perhaps even excessive, respect for the complexities of problems of historical causation, but only in order to justify his own failure to assess the part of the aggressor nations in causing the Second World War. Thereafter Beard proceeds in the remainder of that book and throughout his second one to make a masterpiece of oversimplification in order to lay responsibility for war upon Roosevelt.

Besides excluding material essential for the understanding of Roosevelt's foreign policy, Beard violently distorts the material he does use. His principal distortions are two: that internationalists, led by Roosevelt during the thirties, wanted the United States to go to war; and that Roosevelt practiced deception on the American people regarding the nature and aims of his foreign policy. . . .

Grew Proposes "Constructive Conciliation"

The most important comment, during the whole period, on the Roosevelt-Hull conduct of negotiations with Japan was made on September 29 by Ambassador Grew in a report to Secretary Hull. This report raised the question whether there was not a vista open to the Roosevelt administration located somewhere between the road of appeasement and the road of refusal to appease which might end in war. . . .

In conclusion Grew gave his opinion that the United States would not reach its objective by insisting in preliminary conversations that Japan provide "the sort of clear-cut, specific commitments which appear in any final, formal convention or treaty." Confidence must be placed in the good faith of Konoye and his supporters

to mould Japan's future policy upon the basic principles they are ready to accept and then to adopt measures which gradually but loyally implement those principles, with it understood that the United States will implement its own commitments *pari passu* with the steps Japan takes. . . .

This was what Grew meant by "constructive conciliation," and it was, he asserted, the only alternative to wholesale military defeat of Japan. The Ambassador ended by deferring to "the much broader field of view of President Rossevelt and Secretary Hull," and he expressed "full awareness" that his own approach was "limited to the viewpoint of the American Embassy in Japan."[1]

Secretary Hull makes no reference in his *Memoirs* to this significant report. It must engage the attention of anyone attempting to judge the Roosevelt-Hull policy. In the absence of comment by Hull, it may nevertheless be ventured to estimate his and Roosevelt's view of Grew's proposal on the basis of their known actions and general views. Hull

[1] *Foreign Relations: Japan*, II, 645–50. Also in Grew, *Ten Years in Japan*, 436–42.

in close contact with Roosevelt prepared a comprehensive statement to the Japanese government which he handed to Nomura on October 2. It amounted to an answer to Grew.[2]

Grew's proposal for "constructive conciliation" was vitiated by a basic error of fact. Roosevelt and Hull did not refuse to hold the meeting with Konoye because, as Grew stated in his report, the Japanese failed to provide beforehand "the sort of clear-cut, specific commitments which appear in any final, formal convention or treaty," or because "moderates" in the Japanese government could not "define its future assurances and commitments more specifically than hitherto stated" for fear of pro-German officials. The Japanese government in its communications of September 6 and 22 had satisfied Roosevelt's and Hull's request for preliminary statements of its attitudes and purposes. Roosevelt and Hull refused to hold the meeting with Konoye for a quite different reason, namely, that *the Japanese proposals were unacceptable as a basis for agreement.* They meant nothing else than United States appeasement of Japan, which Grew himself had ruled out as a possible policy for the United States. In fact, they meant more than appeasement; they required United States cooperation with Japan in aggression.

Grew in his report emphasized Japan's agreement to American general principles for peace in the Pacific. He ignored the fact that the practical measures Japan proposed transformed those principles into their opposites. Grew asked Roosevelt and Hull to have faith that the Japanese government would adopt measures which would "gradually but loyally" implement those principles. But Konoye's first step in implementing them was to destroy them and ask the United States to help install opposite principles. If Roosevelt had met Konoye on the basis of the Japanese proposals, he himself would have been guilty of bad faith had he then refused to sign an agreement with Konoye to implement United States cooperation with Japan in aggression. . . .

The Last Chance?

The coming to power of Tojo ended talk of a meeting between Roosevelt and the Japanese Premier. The administration in its efforts to maintain the secrecy of the negotiations, efforts insisted upon by the Japanese who feared the effects of publicity in rousing the militarists,[3] had publicly denied that Prince Konoye had "invited" Roosevelt to a Pacific conference. It was true that the stage of issuing an invitation was never reached. Beard treats the administration's uncommunicativeness as part of its plot to deceive the public by maintaining false "appearances."[4] In his exposition of the "realities" of the affair, Beard declares that Roosevelt and Hull not only pursued the "usual policy" of secrecy, but employed "dilatory" methods. Ambassador Grew's arguments in favor of "constructive conciliation" are Beard's chief evidence in support of his implication that Roosevelt and Hull wanted no reasonable settlement with Japan. But it is noteworthy that after carefully implanting in his reader's mind suspicion that Roosevelt and Hull deliberately rejected a reasonable opportunity for a settlement with Japan, Beard disclaims responsibility for arousing such suspicion by remarking that sufficient documents are not available for judgment. He admits that it is possible to find bases for argument *for,* as well as against Roosevelt's refusal to meet Konoye. Beard

---

[2] *Memoirs of Cordell Hull,* II, 1033. *Foreign Relations: Japan,* II, 656–61.

[3] *Ibid.,* 1024.
[4] Beard, *Roosevelt,* 189–92.

excuses his own failure to use the documents that are available because the "'solution' of this insoluble 'problem'" lay outside the "purposes and limitations" of his book. After calling the Roosevelt-Konoye affair "momentous in the history of American relations with Japan," Beard's evasion of the problem, which would seem to be no more insoluble and is far more adequately documented than most of the problems he claims to solve, is disappointing.[5]

Perhaps Beard had been discouraged by the statement in the Minority Report of the Pearl Harbor Joint Committee, that to go into the issue of the wisdom of the Roosevelt administration in its conduct of relations with Japan,

would involve the committee in the complexities of history extending back more than 50 years and in matters of opinion which cannot be settled by reference to anything as positive and definite as the Constitution, laws, and established administrative practices of the United States government.[6]

Besides, the question was excluded by the terms of the Committee's instructions. But the Committee did not fail to develop information on the subject in order to "understand the questions involved."

Morgenstern, more bold than Beard, examined evidence found by the Committee and other documents, and came to very clear conclusions. "Diplomacy," he writes, "failed because diplomacy was not employed to avert war but to make certain its coming." His chief "evidence" is that administration officials were aware that imposition of economic sanctions against Japan involved a risk that Japan would use force to obtain the raw materials it needed. This is certainly true, but it is a long distance from this to the state-ment that the administration imposed sanctions *because* the policy contained a risk of war. Morgenstern set out to prove more: that the Roosevelt administration made *certain* that war would result.

Perhaps one example of Morgenstern's interpretations will suffice to illustrate his extreme version of the isolationist thesis regarding the Roosevelt-Konoye meeting. He writes that Hull's statement to Nomura that preliminary terms would be discussed with China, Britain, and the Netherlands "demonstrated unmistakably that this country already had an alliance, admitted or not, with China and the western imperialisms and was conducting its diplomacy much more with the view to protecting their interests than its own." Hull's actual purpose was to assure China, Britain, and the Netherlands that the United States would not betray to Japan their rights or territories. The American policy involved was anti-appeasement, which had been proclaimed time and again by Roosevelt and Hull as a policy designed primarily to serve the self-interest of the United States.[7] Incidentally Beard, although he approved Morgenstern's book, found in the documents reason to "put a stop to the vulgar saying: 'The United States was raking British chestnuts out of the fire.'"[8]

It cannot be admitted that with Konoye's fall the last chance of avoiding war with Japan disappeared. If the Roosevelt administration had been willing to support Japan's past and future program of agression, the Tojo government would very likely have been happy to drop the plan to attack the United States, at least temporarily. The actions of Roosevelt and Hull lead one to assume that they believed the risk of new Japanese aggressions was preferable to a profoundly im-

[5] *Ibid.*, 190, 496–506.
[6] JCC, *Report of the Joint Committee, Minority Report*, 497.

[7] Morgenstern, *Pearl Harbor*, 128, 139–40.
[8] Beard, *Roosevelt*, 504n.

moral Far Eastern Munich. History had proved that appeasement was not only immoral but also that aggressors could not be permanently appeased. The most that could have been accomplished by a Far Eastern Munich was to postpone a little longer new Japanese aggressions. This was no temptation for Roosevelt and Hull because it would be then more than balanced by the degradation of the American and all free peoples, because it would violate the American commitment in the Lend Lease Act to aid peaceful nations against aggression, and because it was in any case politically impossible: the great majority of the American people long since had given up indifference to immorality in international relations. . . .

The Wrong Foot

Another grave accusation of the isolationists is that Roosevelt and Hull so conducted negotiations with Kurusu as to coerce the Japanese into attacking the United States. The assumption is made that if the United States refused to make an agreement with Japan, this amounted to coercion of the Japanese and created a situation in which not the Japanese but Roosevelt and Hull were responsible for the Japanese attack that followed. A necessary corollary of the argument is that Kurusu and the Tojo government did in fact "urgently desire" not merely *an* agreement with the United States but one that should have been accepted by Hull and Roosevelt. Charles A. Beard proves at great length that the Japanese did "urgently desire" *an* agreement, which was doubtless true. If the Tojo government could gain the objectives of its aggressive program with the cooperation of the United States, it is difficult to believe that sheer quixoticism would have led it to reject such an arrangement and risk defeat in war instead. Even this, how-

ever, it may be noted in passing, was the choice of Mussolini when France and Britain offered him his price if he would take it without war.

Beard finds in a Japanese proposal on November 20 for a "truce" or *"modus vivendi"* an opportunity for Hull, knowing that it was Japan's "last effort," that the American Army and Navy needed time for preparations, and that a two-front war should "if humanly possible" be avoided, to use "supreme diplomatic ingenuity," and "supreme statesmanship" to "keep conversations going. . . ." Hull on November 26 rejected the Japanese proposal. In Beard's view, Hull "for reasons which are nowhere explicit" failed the supreme test of his career and answered the Japanese with what Beard calls "an ultimative notice."[9]

It is now possible to state certain facts of the situation which were not available to Beard. They suggest that he was too hasty in condemning Hull's statesmanship without sufficient data regarding the possibility that it was Japanese statesmanship, or lack of it, that was responsible for the failure of diplomacy and outbreak of war. After the war, the International Military Tribunal for the Far East found in the Japanese archives the story of Japanese purposes and plans. On November 5, an Imperial Conference decided that if the United States did not accept Japan's terms by November 25 (later extended to November 29), Japan would attack the United States. On November 10, the task force which had been organized and trained to bomb Pearl Harbor was ordered to the Kurile Islands and the date of December 7 was fixed for the attack. On November 22, the task force was ordered to proceed from the Kuriles to Hawaii. These actions were taken *before Hull answered Japan's "last offer"* of

[9] *Ibid.*, 506–16.

November 20. Foreign Minister Togo described the Japanese terms of November 20 as an "ultimatum."[10]

In short, Beard's mistake is that he puts the shoe on the wrong foot. Hull was incapable of issuing an "ultimative notice" to the Japanese after November 20 for the reason that Japan had already issued an ultimatum to the United States on that date, and proceeded to carry out its military threat within two days, before Hull answered its diplomatic threat. Beard would make the Roosevelt administration appear guilty of an aggression in diplomacy which he believes "explains," if it does not excuse, the subsequent Japanese aggression at Pearl Harbor. Actually it was Japan that was guilty of diplomatic as well as military aggression against the United States. Hull knew from Magic intercepts that the Japanese proposals of November 20 constituted an ultimatum involving demands, a deadline, and threat of attack. The only thing he did not know was that the attack was directed at Pearl Harbor or any American territory.

The Modus Vivendi

The Japanese on November 20 offered a draft proposal for a "temporary agreement." In the light of the rejection by the Japanese government, on November 19, of Nomura's suggestion in favor of such an agreement, this proposal must be regarded as the sheerest of hypocrisies designed to occupy the time while the Japanese task force proceeded to Hawaii. Two of the chief issues on which the United States desired settlement, namely, Japan's obligation under the Axis alliance, and economic policy in China and the Pacific regions, were left for later consideration. On remaining issues, Japan offered to make one concession, withdrawal of Japanese troops from southern

to northern Indo-China, in return for United States cooperation with Japan in securing the fruits of aggression in China. Japan asked the United States to stop giving aid to China and to restore economic relations with Japan, including delivery to Japan of a required quantity of oil, while Japan made "peace" with China. Kurusu had admitted to Hull that "peace" with China would involve the stationing of Japanese troops there for an indefinite period. Besides providing Japan with American oil to help it impose its will on China, the United States was asked to "cooperate" with Japan in obtaining for it oil and other materials in the NEI. Japan would promise to make no armed movement southward, but offered no guaranty against aggression northward.[11]

Hull considered that the proposals called for "virtually a surrender" by the United States. He asked Kurusu and Nomura, as he later wrote:

what they thought would be the public reaction in the United States if we were to announce tomorrow that we had decided to discontinue aid to Great Britain. There was no reply. "In the minds of the American people," I continued, "the purposes underlying our aid to China are the same as the purposes underlying aid to Great Britain. . . ."[12]

Hull regarded the situation as virtually hopeless. But the military leaders pleaded with him for more time, and therefore Hull and State Department officials sought desperately to work out some counterproposal to keep the conversations going. For a few days a three-months' *modus vivendi* was considered. It is noteworthy that it was while Hull worked on this scheme that the Japanese task force was ordered on November 22 to proceed eastward through the north

---

[10] Ballantine, "Mukden to Pearl Harbor," 662–4.

[11] *Foreign Relations: Japan,* II, 748–9, 755–6.
[12] *Memoirs of Cordell Hull,* II, 1070–1.

Pacific to reach Hawaii by December 7. No inkling of this reached American observers or officials in Washington, but ominous movements of Japanese forces into positions where they were poised for attacks against Thailand, Malaya, the NEI, and possibly the Philippines or Guam, were known in detail. On November 24, Army and Navy commanders in the Pacific were warned that a Japanese "surprise aggressive movement in any direction including an attack on the Philippines or Guam is a possibility."[13] This was interpreted in Hawaii to require no change in preparations against sabotage as the chief danger.

President Roosevelt, Secretary of the Treasury Morgenthau, and other officials helped Hull explore the possibility of a *modus vivendi*, and he consulted the representatives of Great Britain, China, the Netherlands, and Australia. A Magic intercept from Tokyo to Kurusu and Nomura on November 22 extended the deadline from November 25 to 29. One phrase in it provides the first reason why Hull in the end decided not to make a counterproposal for a *modus vivendi*. The Japanese Ambassadors were instructed: "Stick to our fixed policy. . . ." This could only mean that nothing but complete American surrender to the Japanese proposals would satisfy Tojo. It confirmed Hull's belief that no arrangement that the United States could accept would be acceptable to Japan. The intercepted message ended: "This time we mean it, that the deadline absolutely cannot be changed. After that things are automatically going to happen."[14]

The second reason why Hull decided against the *modus vivendi* is that the government of China objected to it and obtained wide support for its objection, incuding that of Churchill. The final American draft of the *modus vivendi* called for mutual pledges that the United States and Japan would not advance in the Pacific area by force or threat of force; Japan would withdraw its troops from southern Indo-China, and also reduce its forces in northern Indo-China to 25,000—a number thought to preclude a campaign to close the Burma Road; the United States would allow limited quantities of American oil, cotton, and other commodities to go to Japan and it would buy Japanese goods; the United States would urge Britain, Australia, and the Netherlands to resume trade similarly with Japan; and the United States affirmed its fundamental position that any settlement between Japan and China must be based upon the principles of "peace, law, order, and justice." Attached to this three-months' *modus vivendi* was a ten-point proposal for a permanent agreement.[15]

The *modus vivendi* drawn up by Hull meant temporary appeasement of Japan insofar as it would give temporary United States approval to Japanese conquests and relax the economic sanctions which the United States, Britain, Australia and the Netherlands had imposed against Japan during preceding months. The plan must be regarded as a product of the desperation of the Roosevelt administration in its fight for time. Had it been offered to Japan, it would have been a violation of the administration's principle of no compromise with aggression.

Only agreement by China, the government which would be the chief victim of this appeasement, that the time which might be gained would be worth the sacrifice, would have justified such an offer to Japan. China refused to agree.

---

[13] JCC, *Hearings*, Vol. 84, Pt. 14, Exhibit 37, p. 1405.
[14] *Memoirs of Cordell Hull*, II, 1074.

[15] *Ibid.*, 1072–3, 1077–81.

Churchill supported the Chinese view. After hectic discussions, the decision was reached on the night of November 25, to make no counterproposal of a *modus vivendi* but to answer the Japanese only with the ten-point proposal for a permanent settlement.[16]

On the Rock of Principle

In this decision the Roosevelt administration met the supreme test of its statesmanship in service of the policy of collective security against aggression. Beard's statement that the decision was made "for reasons which are nowhere explicit"[17] is nonsense; Beard himself recites the evidence that the Chinese government violently opposed the *modus vivendi*. He ignores another contributing factor, that is, the futility of offering to Japan, in the face of the intercepted instructions to the Ambassadors to "stick to our fixed policy," an American *modus vivendi* which would have required Japan to retreat from its "fixed policy," especially in the matter of the number of troops to be left in northern Indo-China. Beard does not wish to admit that the one thing which might have justified temporary appeasement of Japan was the consent of China. The Roosevelt administration refused to make a deal with Japan affecting China's fate without its consent. It refused to ignore the rights of China as Chamberlain had ignored those of Czechoslovakia at Munich.

On the rock of this principle, the last possibility of Roosevelt and Hull attempting to postpone the deadline in Japan's ultimatum collapsed. Actually, no such possibility existed. But the administration believed that a possibility still existed that Japan would only attack non-American territory, leaving room for a choice by the United States whether it should enter the war.

No one but an absolute pacifist would argue that the danger of war is a greater evil than violation of principle. It must be concluded that the isolationist thesis involves denunciation of the Roosevelt-Hull decision against the *modus vivendi* because of the nature of the principle involved. The isolationist believes that appeasement of Japan without China's consent violated no principle worth a risk of war. The internationalist must believe that the principle did justify a risk of war. In short, subjective and *a priori* attitudes ultimately determine judgment of the Roosevelt-Hull policy. If an observer can be imagined to exist who is "neutral" as between the attitudes of isolationists and internationalists, he might conclude that it did not matter whether or not the Roosevelt administration offered the *modus vivendi* because the Japanese government was certain to reject it.

A Third Choice?

By means of innuendos rather than overt statement, Beard implies that the Roosevelt administration had a third choice besides appeasement or refusal to appease, and took it: war. He combs the record to find "war-like" statements of the leaders in Washington, and presents them in sinister array entirely out of context. The President and his Cabinet on November 25, Beard writes, "discussed war, not prospects of peace. . . ." In Beard's vocabulary, discussion of war is synonymous with a desire for war. Secretary Stimson wrote in his diary regarding a meeting of the "War Council" with Roosevelt on November 25, which was attended by him and Hull, Knox, Marshall, and Stark, that Roosevelt brought up the likelihood that the Japanese, notorious for surprise attacks,

---

[16] *Ibid.,* 1074–81.
[17] Beard, *Roosevelt,* 515.

would attack the United States within two days:

and the question was what we should do. The question was how we should maneuver them into the position of firing the first shot without allowing too much danger to ourselves. It was a difficult proposition.

Beard quotes this and Stimson's later amplification to the Joint Congressional Committee:

In spite of the risk involved, however, in letting the Japanese fire the first shot, we realized that in order to have the full support of the American people it was desirable to make sure that the Japanese be the ones to do this so that there should remain no doubt in anyone's mind as to who were the aggressors.

These, and many variations of the theme in discussions in Washington, Beard assembles to suggest that the administration wanted war with Japan. He entitles his final chapter, dealing with the outbreak of war: "Maneuvering the Japanese into Firing the First Shot."[18]

The part of the Japanese government in maneuvering itself into firing the first shot is not discussed by Beard. The situation as he describes it leads a reader to believe that it was the United States that took the initiative for war during the weeks preceding December 7, while Japan was coerced into beginning a war it had sought to avoid. Stimson's word "maneuver" is magnified out of all relation to the actual position of the two governments in which Japan, of course, exercised the initiative and the United States was forced into a war it had sought to avoid. After creating suspicion in the reader's mind that Stimson and the other leaders knew that the Japanese intended to attack Pearl Harbor, and that they wanted the attack to occur, Beard makes

Stimson's use of the word "maneuver" appear to have been an affirmation of the administration's knowledge and desire. But, as has been shown, the administration thought exclusively in terms of a Japanese movement southward. The question was whether the President should ask Congress for a declaration of war *prior* to a Japanese attack on the Philippines or Guam, in order to avoid giving Japan the advantage of a surprise attack, or wait until Japan attacked United States territory, that is, "maneuver" Japan into firing the first shot. Despite much discussion, no final decision to ask Congress for a declaration of war was made. The other course, waiting while Japan might attack the United States, was a "maneuver" only in the sense that it involved avoidance of any action that would make the United States even *seem* to provoke or justify an attack by Japan. Whereas Beard makes the word appear to mean that the administration took positive actions to coerce the Japanese into attacking, it actually meant that the United States should do nothing that would give Japan an excuse for war.

The Southward Expedition

Beard calls the United States reply on November 26 to the Japanese proposal of November 20 an "ultimative notice." Morgenstern calls it more simply an "ultimatum."[19] The Minority Report of the Joint Congressional Committee declares that Japan "treated" the answer "as an ultimatum," and that Hull on November 28, if not on November 26, knew that it would so treat it.[20] Dramatic proof came on November 25 that it was Japan that had not only issued an ultimatum on November 20 but proceeded to carry out its new program of aggression without

---

[18] *Ibid.*, 517–9 ff.

[19] Morgenstern, *Pearl Harbor*, 288 *et passim*.
[20] JCC, *Minority Report*, 563–4.

waiting for an answer from the United States. On the afternoon of the 25th, intelligence reports to Secretary Stimson stated that five Japanese divisions were moving southwards from Shantung and Shansi towards Indo-China or points beyond.[21] If more evidence were needed by the administration that the Japanese government had no intention of accepting any *modus vivendi* or any arrangement that would inhibit its program of conquest, this provided it. The President and Hull were sent copies of the report. Morgenstern avoids assessing this intelligence report at its face value by noting that on the next day, when Hull discussed with Stimson his decision to reject the *modus vivendi*, he "did not refer to the Japanese troop movement." Morgenstern notes that when the President on the 26th heard of the troop movement from Stimson, he said it "changed the whole situation, because it was an evidence of bad faith on the part of the Japanese. . . ." But, writes Morgenstern, the Hull answer to Japan that day had already "changed the whole situation."[22]

The United States was actually incapable of "changing the whole situation" no matter what it did short of an attack against Japan, and even this in the circumstances would have been an offensive action only on the level of tactics: Japan had already seized the initiative of the offensive on the higher level of strategy. The Japanese aggressive movement southward was obviously launched well before the Japanese government expected any reply to its proposal of a *modus vivendi*. News of it in Washington merely *confirmed* one of the premises upon which the decision was made to reject the *modus vivendi*: that Japan acted in bad faith. Beyond this, it is clear now

that Japan was willing to expose its bad faith by moving an expedition southward in plain view because it served as a screen for its more stunning act of bad faith in sending the expedition to Pearl Harbor.

Considering the scope of Japanese bad faith, what was hidden from Washington as well as what was exposed, one may call suspicion of Japan, which was the fundamental source of Chinese and all other opposition to the *modus vivendi*, the highest statesmanship. Had the *modus vivendi* been accepted, the lowering of guard and injury to morale among all anti-Axis peoples and governments would have invited disaster much more severe than actually occurred. Japan in its diplomacy and its military actions had already launched new aggressions against every Pacific power before the United States had an opportunity to accept or reject the *modus vivendi*. To search in such a situation for ignorance among Washington officials of the full scope of Japanese aggression in order to fix war guilt on them is ludicrous, especially in view of the charge by the same critics that Washington officials should have been more suspicious than they were of Japanese intentions at Pearl Harbor.

Even if Hull's November 26 answer to Japan had been an ultimatum, it would have been a nullity because Japan had issued one earlier and was acting on it. While it is conceivable that the orders to the Pearl Harbor expedition, and even the southward expedition, could have been rescinded during the days that remained prior to December 7, it is still true that the very act of sending those expeditions in the directions of their respective targets while "negotiations" proceeded in Washington constituted a threat of war signifying not merely bad faith but that those negotiations took

[21] JCC, *Hearings*, Vol. 83, Pt. 11, pp. 5433–4.
[22] Morgenstern, *Pearl Harbor*, 288.

place under the sanction of a Japanese ultimatum.

The Message of November 26

Hull's answer on November 26 was a refusal to surrender to the Japanese ultimatum. This was implicit in his rejection of the Japanese proposal for a *modus vivendi*. But he did not entirely reject that proposal, and he offered Japan a draft plan for an agreement on all points at issue as a basis for continued negotiations. This took away from his answer all character of a challenge to Japan to carry out its threat of war. Hull did not expect the Japanese government to accept his constructive proposal for an agreement, and he warned the armed service chiefs that Japan could be expected now to attack, but this was not, as the isolationists charge, proof that he regarded his answer as an "ultimatum." It was proof that he judged correctly that Japan would attack if the United States did not entirely surrender to Japan's ultimatum.

Hull's draft proposal for an American-Japanese agreement contained ten points. None of them was unacceptable or disadvantageous to a Japanese government mindful of the real interests of Japan: 1) a multilateral nonaggression pact among the governments principally concerned in the Pacific; 2) an agreement among the governments principally interested to respect the territorial integrity of Indo-China and equality of economic opportunity in that country; 3) no support of any Chinese government except the national government of Chiang Kai-shek; 4) relinquishment of extraterritorial rights in China by the United States as well as all other powers; 5) a liberal trade agreement between the United States and Japan; 6) mutual removal of freezing measures; 7) stabilization of currency values between the dollar and the yen;

8) an agreement that neither country would interpret an agreement with a third country in a way that would conflict with the fundamental purpose of establishing peace; 9) both governments would use their influence to lead other governments to accept and carry out the principles of this American-Japanese agreement; 10) Japan would withdraw its forces from China and Indo-China.

This draft proposal was accompanied by an explanation that the United States government regarded "some" but not all of the points in the Japanese *modus vivendi* of November 20 as in conflict with the fundamental principles to which each government had committed itself. The American draft proposal was not offered as the only terms of agreement the United States was willing to accept. Hull explained to Nomura and Kurusu that it was offered as "*one practical exemplification of a program which this Government envisages as something to be worked out during our further conversations.*"[23]

To sum up: the American answer to Japan on November 26 did not reject *all* of the terms of Japan's proposed *modus vivendi;* the American draft proposal was not offered as the *only* terms of agreement the United States would accept; the United States made *no* demands upon Japan; the American draft proposal contained many offers that the Japanese had often admitted were advantageous to Japan because they would satisfy Japanese demands for security and prosperity —most significantly, an offer to end United States economic sanctions against Japan; it named *no deadline* for an answer by Japan; it contained *no threat of force or war* or other penalty if Japan refused to accept the American proposal; it specifically *invited* Japan to *continue*

[23] *Foreign Relations: Japan,* II, 764–70. Italics added.

negotiations; it *promised to consider* new Japanese proposals, in the usual manner of a peaceful power, in the course of further negotiations.

To call such a proposal an "ultimatum" or an "ultimative notice" is to murder the meaning of the word. If, as the Minority Report asserts, the Japanese war lords "treated" this answer "as an ultimatum," evidence is available, in Togo's description of the Japanese terms of November 20 as an ultimatum, which proves that he, at least, had for some days already accepted the fact which American isolationists reject: that to the Japanese government belonged the responsibility for war that accrues to a government guilty of issuing an ultimatum. When the Japanese Foreign Minister admits responsibility, it seems excessive for Americans to find the Japanese innocent and their own government guilty.

Elting E. Morison:
AN UNANSWERABLE QUESTION

Elting E. Morison is professor of history at Massachusetts Institute of Technology, winner of the J. H. Dunning Prize of the American Historical Association for a biography of Admiral Sims, and well-known for his eight-volume edition of the letters of Theodore Roosevelt. In the following selection, taken from his biography of Henry L. Stimson, Turmoil and Tradition, *Morison draws conclusions about the role of Roosevelt's Secretary of War in the coming of the conflict. This and the next several selections differ from the preceding ones in being more concerned with responsibility for the surprise achieved by the Japanese at Pearl Harbor than with the general direction of American policy.*

YET the end had come in such a way that there were questions. Some of these questions were left until the war that began at Pearl Harbor was over. It was then asked whether the Roosevelt Administration had not tried, as the sole object of its negotiations in 1941, to put us into a war in the Pacific that would get us into the war in Europe. It was even asked whether, in pursuit of this purpose, Pearl Harbor had not been somehow planned that way. Had not officials in Washington deliberately withheld "practically all of the vital information concerning the developing Japanese situation" from the commanders in Hawaii? There is nothing to say about the allegations implicit in these questions except that they are not true.

The administration had three objectives in its negotiations with Japan in 1941. It sought to divide the Axis powers that had signed the pact of September 27, 1940; to prevent the expansion of Japanese power in Southeast Asia; to restore all the things that are meant by the Open Door in China. Evidence is available to suggest that the administration had considerable success in obtaining the first two objectives—on which immediate

From Turmoil and Tradition by Elting E. Morison. (Boston, Houghton Mifflin Company, 1960.) Pp. 530–537. Reprinted with permission of the publisher.

peace in the Pacific depended—until July 1941. Then, it has been said, by insisting on the third objective, by hardening its heart in defense of all those moralities that had accumulated about the idea of the Open Door, the administration lost its previous advantages. Unwilling to modify this "morally inspired position," increasingly inflexible in the defense of it, the administration thus crowded the Japanese into a position from which they could only fight back. War, in other words, might well have been avoided if the administration had proceeded in elastic negotiation to adjust the immediate necessities; if it had not proved intransigent on the ultimate intention to free China. No one knows. It can be argued that given time and elastic negotiation the immediate difficulties between Japan and the United States could have been resolved. Ambassador Joseph C. Grew so argued and he was on the spot at the time. It can and should be argued, as George Kennan does, that sentiment and a fixed conviction of moral duty are in themselves inadequate bases for a foreign policy. It can be argued that nothing in the previous ten years of Japanese history gave much if any promise that the country, any more than Hitler's Germany, would respond favorably to elastic negotiation. What would have happened if things had been done differently must be, in the light of all the variables, an unanswered question.[1]

[1] The most reasoned and sensible statement of the position described in this paragraph is to be found in Paul W. Schroeder, *The Axis Alliance and Japanese-American Relations, 1941* (Ithaca, 1958), 200–216. . . . In this same connection one should also read the imaginative book by Robert E. Osgood, *Ideals and Self-Interest in America's Foreign Relations* (Chicago, 1953). In speaking of the beginning of our modern troubles with Japan—Manchuria—he says (352–53) that we should either have decided that Japan's action was both a breach of morality and a danger to our national interest, in which

But from the things that were done the war came. Stimson had a hand in these things. From the very beginning, before most others in political office at the time, he had believed in the firm rather than the elastic response. He believed in this for two reasons. First, his understanding of history and his personal recollections convinced him that Japan would yield only to direct pressures. Second, he believed that what was involved in the East was not only national interest but principle, the underlying moralities of the thing. On such matters, whatever the consequences, there could be in his mind no compromise.

With these larger questions there were also others which had to do with the immediate event. To what extent, for instance, were those in Washington responsible for what had happened at Pearl Harbor? On this matter of general or collective responsibility the Secretary of War said, "No one in Washington had correctly assessed Japanese intentions and capabilities." He, "like everyone else," had been "painfully surprised by the skill and boldness displayed by all

case we should have used strong measures not excluding force, or we should have decided Japan's action did not endanger our interests, in which case regular diplomatic devices would have served. In the event, what we did was to take a vigorous moral stand without regard to the practical consequences. The measures taken were "pitifully inadequate" while the public was encouraged to believe in their adequacy "in accordance with the wishful supposition that world opinion alone could alter basic power conflicts." Somewhat the same rigidity was at work, in Schroeder's opinion, in 1941. My own view is that, all things considered, it is probable that no attempt at accommodation, no set of elastic negotiations, would have prevented Japan's continued threatening expansion in Asia until, in time, it reached some vital American interest like the Philippines. For ten years the country had taken advantage of every opportunity offered. This is not to say that the Western powers had acted wisely at all times in their dealings with Japan in those ten years.

branches of the Japanese war machine from December 7 onward." Moreover, "Washington had not adequately appreciated the importance of keeping its field commanders fully informed." And, finally when the majority report of the Joint Committee of Congress to investigate Pearl Harbor "by no means exonerated War Department officials, . . . the responsibility which it inferentially placed on him, as head of the War Department, he was quite willing to accept."[2]

Beyond responsibilities collective and inferential there was also a possible responsibility individual and particular. Of all the countless causes of this remarkable disaster, one certainly was that Pearl Harbor on that Sunday morning lay at Alert Number 1. It lay, in other words, in the standard defense against sabotage "with no threat from without." The fact was that General Short had misinterpreted the message designed to put all the Pacific commands on "the qui vive for any attack."

For this misinterpretation was he himself alone responsible? An Army board of investigation in 1944 thought not. The board members held that the "final alert" of November 27 was in its phrasing ambiguous. They called it the "Do-Don't message." They also believed that General Short's reply stating that he had alerted his department to prevent sabotage should have revealed to the War Department the extent of the General's misunderstanding, especially since, on the basis of existing information, "positive directives could have been formulated to put the [Hawaiian] Department on Alert Number 3." Reviewing these points, the board members concluded

that "The difference between alerting those defenses in time by a directive from the War Department based upon this information and the failure to alert them is a difference for which the War Department is responsible, wholly aside from Short's responsibility in not himself having selected the right alert."[3]

Who then, in the War Department, was responsible for this difference? General Gerow was the head of the War Plans Division which had actually sent out the final alert of November 27. He had taken a hand in framing the alert. He had seen General Short's reply. When he failed to recognize in this reply that General Short had misinterpreted the message of November 27 and thus had taken no corrective step, he had been, he later said, "in error."[4]

The Secretary of War had, in his conversation with President Roosevelt, been the instigator of this final alert. He too had taken a hand in framing the message. He had actually written some of the words that were said to contribute most to the ambiguity of the alert. Had he also, therefore, been "in error"? Was he in some sort a sharer in the direct responsibility assigned by the Army Pearl Harbor Board to the War Department?

There were, of course, extenuating circumstances. The Do-Don't message was no more ambiguous than the times. It did describe the situation quite precisely. Of all the commanding generals in the Pacific, only General Short misconstrued its meaning as far as the setting of the alerts was concerned. In the ordinary course of events the Secretary of War would have taken no part in the com-

[2] Mark Watson, *U. S. Army in World War II, the War Department, Chief of Staff: prewar plans and preparations* (Washington 1950).

[3] *Pearl Harbor Hearings,* Part 3, p. 1035; *Supplement to the General Report of the Army Pearl Harbor Board,* 1–2.
[4] Watson, *Chief of Staff,* 509.

position of the message. He did so only because General Marshall was away on troop maneuvers. Also, in the ordinary course of departmental procedure he would not have been expected to take action upon receiving General Short's unsatisfactory reply. It was routine for him to initial a copy of this reply but it was also routine for the War Plans Division, as the originator of the first message, to deal with Short's response.

These were some of the extenuating circumstances. Yet, given all the facts, a prosecutor less experienced than Stimson would have little trouble in convincing a jury that the Secretary had started something he did not wholly finish, that in so doing he contributed directly to the "difference between alerting those defenses in time by a directive from the War Department . . . and the failure to alert them," and that for this difference he was, therefore, in some part responsible. This is a finding never explicitly stated in an official report. But the line of argument, once started, does not appear to lead to any other conclusion.

The Secretary of War had a different view. He felt, to begin with—and with much justification—that the message of November 27 "presented with the utmost precision the situation with which we were all confronted. . . ." Therefore, "we assumed that when [General Short] had been [thus] warned . . . it would not be necessary to repeat that warning over and over again during the ensuing days." And quite apart from this was the position of General Short as an outpost commander. He was "like a sentinel on duty in the face of the enemy." It was not his "to speculate or rely on the possibilities of the enemy attacking at some other outpost instead of his own. It is his duty to meet him at his post at any

time and to make the best possible fight that can be made against him with the weapons with which he has been supplied." In this duty, he concluded, "the commanders in Hawaii failed."[5]

This view excluded the Secretary of War from any part of the responsibility for the direct consequences of the message of November 27. The analogy between the outpost commander and the sentinel is not, perhaps, wholly exact; the explanation given will not, probably, satisfy everyone. It has in fact been suggested that Stimson took this view from one of a variety of motives: because in so doing he could protect General Marshall from attack for the errors of his subordinates; because he was in this way "passing the buck" to an officer in the field; because he could save himself from blame. Nothing is beyond all doubt in the domain of motive. It is conceivable that in some deep, private recess, concealed from himself and others, he found it impossible, after all his schooling in the imperatives of duty, to believe that a duty left unperformed might be a duty of his own and thus he displaced his share of responsibility on others. But the less recondite explanation appears the more correct. He believed what he said. Nothing in his whole career suggests that on such a matter he could possibly have done otherwise. Those who knew him best, who saw him at the time, who talked with him afterwards, have no doubts on this subject. Concerning the message of November 27 and the position of General Short, he simply thought he was right.[6]

[5] *Active Service*, 392; *Pearl Harbor Hearings*, Part II, pp. 5424–25, 5428–29.
[6] Current, *Secretary Stimson*, 188. On page 391 of *Active Service* Stimson speaks of the "preposterous charge" made in the Army Pearl Harbor Board report that General Marshall himself might bear some of the responsibility for Gen-

It is inevitable that in the individual interest efforts should be made to personify the causes and quantify the responsibilities for Pearl Harbor. But such efforts have done little to reveal why things turned out as they did. The misapprehension of General Short is still only a single item in what is apparently an inexplicable sequence: The massive miscalculation of the Japanese intention by all those in high authority, the ar-

rival of the unarmed B-17's, the submerged submarine detected at the harbor gate at 0350 hours, the morning ride of General Marshall, the unregarded message from the mobile radar unit that picked up the track of Japanese planes 132 miles from Oahu, and all those other things right down to the boy, the undelivered telegram and the bicycle. Not even a system schemed out in total depravity to produce all the wrong things at all the wrong times could have organized such compounding error and misfortune. As Robert Sherwood said, "Millions of words have been recorded by at least eight official investigating bodies and one may read through all of them without arriving at an adequate explanation of why, with war so obviously ready to break out *somewhere* in the Pacific, our principal Pacific base was in a condition of peacetime Sunday morning somnolence instead of in Condition Red. . . ."[7]

---

eral Short's failures. To offset the effects of this report Stimson himself started an investigation of his own conducted by Lieutenant Colonel Clausen. Clausen's report, consisting principally of interviews with and affidavits from various officers involved in the Pearl Harbor attack, though massive, does not in fact clear up any of the real issues left unclear by the official investigations. The Proceedings of the Army Pearl Harbor Board are reprinted in *Pearl Harbor Hearings*, Parts 27, 28, 29, 30, 31. Stimson's testimony before this Board is given in Part 29, pp. 2063–87. An account which includes much of this testimony and which gives an unfavorable interpretation of Stimson's actions, both before and after, in connection with Pearl Harbor is found in Current, *Secretary Stimson*, Ch. 8.

[7] Sherwood, *Roosevelt and Hopkins*, 434.

Husband E. Kimmel: ADMIRAL KIMMEL'S STORY

The commander of the Pacific Fleet at the time of the surprise attack presents his own defence in this selection from Admiral Kimmel's Story. He cites deficiencies in the military establishment that stemmed from public neglect, political commitments of which he was not informed, and specifies those things known to various levels of the United States government of which he was left unaware, purposely or otherwise.

ALTHOUGH the commanders at Hawaii were never supplied with the equipment and trained personnel to decode intercepted "magic" Japanese dispatches, I learned during the investigations in Washington that the com-

mander-in-chief of our Asiatic Fleet was fully equipped to decode the "magic" intercepted Japanese dispatches as received; also that the Navy Department in Washington maintained a check system and supplied the Asiatic decoding

Reprinted by permission from *Admiral Kimmel's Story* by Husband E. Kimmel. Copyright 1955. Henry Regnery Company, Chicago. Pp. 82–3, 86–7, 89, 92–3, 94, 98–9, 107–11.

unit with copies of important intercepts which the organization failed to obtain with their own facilities. I also learned that a fourth set of equipment destined for assignment to the commander-in-chief, U.S. Pacific Fleet, at Hawaii was diverted to the British in the summer of 1941. The Navy and War Departments in Washington were each supplied with equipment and personnel to decode their intercepts.

The care taken to keep the commander-in-chief of our Asiatic Fleet and the British in London informed of Japanese intentions while withholding this vital information from our commanders at Pearl Harbor has never been explained.

In the month of July, 1941, the Chief of Naval Operations sent me at least seven dispatches which quoted intercepted Japanese diplomatic messages from Tokyo to Washington, Tokyo to Berlin, Berlin to Tokyo, Tokyo to Vichy, Canton to Tokyo. These dispatches identified by number the Japanese messages they quoted and gave their verbatim text.

I was never informed of any decision to the effect that intelligence from intercepted Japanese messages was not to be sent to me. In fact, dispatches sent to me by the Navy Department in the week before the attack contained intelligence from intercepted messages. On December 1, a dispatch from the Chief of Naval Operations, sent to me for information, quoted a report of November 29 from the Japanese ambassador in Bangkok to Tokyo which described a Japanese plan to entice the British to invade Thai, thereby permitting Japan to enter that country in the role of its defender. On December 3, a dispatch to me from the Chief of Naval Operations set forth an order from Japan to diplomatic agents and expressly referred

to this order as "Circular Twenty Four Forty Four from Tokyo." Another dispatch from the Chief of Naval Operations on December 3 referred to certain "categoric and urgent instructions which were sent yesterday to Japanese diplomatic and consular posts."

The Navy Department thus engaged in a course of conduct which definitely gave me the impression that intelligence from important intercepted Japanese messages was being furnished to me. Under these circumstances a failure to send me important information of this character was not merely a withholding of intelligence. It amounted to an affirmative misrepresentation. I had asked for all vital information. I had been assured that I would have it. I appeared to be receiving it. My current estimate of the situation was formed on this basis. Yet, in fact, the most vital information from the intercepted Japanese messages was withheld from me. This failure not only deprived me of essential facts. It misled me.

I was not supplied with any information of the intercepted messages showing that the Japanese government had divided Pearl Harbor into five areas and was seeking minute information as to the berthing of ships of the fleet in those areas which were vitally significant. . . .

In the volume of intercepted Japanese dispatches eliciting and securing information about American military installations and naval movements, the dispatches concerning Pearl Harbor, on and after September 24, 1941, stand out, apart from the others. No other harbor or base in American territory or possessions was divided into sub-areas by Japan. In no other area was the Japanese government seeking information as to whether two or more vessels were alongside the same wharf. Prior to the dispatch of September 24, the information which the Japanese sought and obtained about Pearl Harbor followed the general pattern of their interest in American fleet movements in other localities. One might expect this type of conventional espionage.

With the dispatch of September 24, 1941, and those which followed, there was a significant and ominous change in the character of the information which the Japanese government sought and obtained. The espionage then directed was of an unusual character and outside the realm of reasonable suspicion. It was no longer merely directed to ascertaining the general whereabouts of ships of the fleet. It was directed to the presence of particular ships in particular areas; to such minute detail as what ships were double-docked at the same wharf.

In the period immediately preceding the attack, the Jap consul general in Hawaii was directed by Tokyo to report even when there were no movements of ships in and out of Pearl Harbor. These Japanese instructions and reports pointed to an attack by Japan upon the ships in Pearl Harbor. The information sought and obtained, with such painstaking detail, had no other conceivable usefulness from a military viewpoint. Its utility was in planning and executing an attack upon ships in port. Its effective value was lost completely when the ships left their reported berthings in Pearl Harbor.

No one had a more direct and immediate interest in the security of the fleet in Pearl Harbor than its commander-in-chief. No one had a greater right than I to know that Japan had carved up Pearl Harbor into sub-areas and was seeking and receiving reports as to the precise berthings in that harbor of the ships of the fleet. I had been sent Mr. Grew's report earlier in the year with positive

advice from the Navy Department that no credence was to be placed in the rumored Japanese plans for an attack on Pearl Harbor. I was told then, that no Japanese move against Pearl Harbor appeared "imminent or planned for in the foreseeable future." Certainly I was entitled to know when information in the Navy Department completely altered the information and advice previously given to me. Surely, I was entitled to know of the intercepted dispatches between Tokyo and Honolulu on and after September 24, 1941, which indicated that a Japanese move against Pearl Harbor was planned in Tokyo. . . .

The intercepted dispatches about the berthings of ships in Pearl Harbor also clarified the significance of other intercepted Japanese dispatches, decoded and translated by the Navy Department prior to the attack. I refer particularly to the intercepted dispatches which established a deadline date for agreement between Japan and the United States. When this date passed without agreement, these dispatches revealed that a Japanese plan automatically took effect. . . .

In at least six separate dispatches, on November 5, 11, 15, 16, 22, and 24, Japan specifically established and extended the deadline of November 25, later advanced to November 29. The dispatches made it plain that after the deadline date a Japanese plan was automatically going into operation. The plan was of such importance that, as the deadline approached, the government of Japan declared: "The fate of our Empire hangs by the slender thread of a few days."

When the deadline date of November 29 was reached with no agreement between the United States and Japan, there was no further extension. The intercepted dispatches indicated that the crisis deepened in its intensity after that day passed. On the first of December, Tokyo advised its ambassadors in Washington: "The date set in my message No. 812 has come and gone and the situation continues to be increasingly critical." This message was translated by the navy on the first of December. This information was never supplied to me.

An intercepted Japanese dispatch from Tokyo to Washington of November 28, 1941, made it clear that the American proposal of November 26 was completely unsatisfactory to Japan and that an actual rupture of negotiations would occur upon the receipt of the Japanese reply. A dispatch on November 28, decoded and translated on the same day, stated:

Well, you two ambassadors have exerted superhuman efforts but, in spite of this, the United States has gone ahead and presented this humiliating proposal. This was quite unexpected and extremely regrettable. The Imperial Government can by no means use it as a basis for negotiations. Therefore, with a report of the views of the Imperial Government on this American proposal which I will send you in two or three days, the negotiations will be de facto ruptured. This is inevitable. . . .

This information was never supplied to me.

The commanders at Pearl Harbor were not kept informed of the progress of negotiations with Japan. I was never supplied with the text of Mr. Hull's message of November 26, 1941 to the Japanese government which has frequently been referred to as an ultimatum. This was a most important document. It stated the policy of the United States that would be carried out by force, if necessary. Mr. Stimson referred to this message as Mr. Hull's decision "to kick the whole thing over. . . ."

The Japanese reply to this message was delivered in Washington within hours of the Japanese attack at Pearl Harbor. Nor were the commanders at Pearl Harbor supplied with the text of previous messages exchanged between the United States and Japanese governments. Their information on this subject was obtained from the radio and newspapers. I now believe that the Washington newspaper correspondents and the editors of our leading newspapers were much more accurately informed of the seriousness of the situation than were the commanders at Pearl Harbor. . . .

After November 27, there was a rising intensity in the crisis in Japanese-United States relations apparent in the intercepted dispatches. I was told on November 27 that negotiations had ceased and two days later that they appeared to be terminated with the barest possibilities of their resumption. Then I was left to read public accounts of further conversations between the State Department and the Japanese emissaries in Washington which indicated that negotiations had been resumed.

The Navy Department knew immediately of the reactions of Nomura and Kurusu to the American note of November 26—"Our failure and humiliation are complete."

The Navy Department knew immediately of the reactions of the Japanese government to the American note of November 26. Japan termed it:

A humiliating proposal. This was quite unexpected and extremely regrettable. The Imperial Government can by no means use it as a basis for negotiations. Therefore with a report of the views of the Imperial Government on this American proposal which I will send you in two or three days, the negotiations will be de facto ruptured. This is inevitable.

The Navy Department knew that Nomura and Kurusu suggested to Japan on November 26 one way of saving the situation—a wire by the President to the Emperor.

The Navy Department knew that the Japanese government advised Nomura and Kurusu on November 28 that the suggested wire from the President to the Emperor offered no hope: "What you suggest is entirely unsuitable."

The Navy Department knew that on November 30, Japan gave Germany a detailed version of the negotiations with the United States. Japan stated that "a continuation of negotiations would inevitably be detrimental to our cause," and characterized certain features of the American proposal of November 26 as "insulting"—"clearly a trick." Japan concluded that the United States had decided to regard her as an enemy.

The Navy Department knew that Japan had instructed her ambassadors in Berlin on November 30 to inform Hitler:

The conversations begun between Tokyo and Washington last April . . . now stand ruptured—broken. Say very secretly to them [Hitler and Ribbentrop] that there is extreme danger that war may suddenly break out between the Anglo-Saxon nations and Japan through some clash of arms and add that the time of the breaking out of this war may come quicker than anyone dreams.

All this vital information came from intercepted dispatches, decoded and translated in Washington, either on the day they were sent or a day or two later. None of this information was supplied to me. . . .

It is one thing to warn commanders at a particular base of the probable outbreak of war in theaters thousands of miles away, knowing and expecting that they will continue their assigned tasks and missions after the receipt of such warning, and that the very nature of the warning emphasizes to them the necessity for continuing such tasks and missions.

It is quite another thing to warn commanders at a particular base of an attack to be expected in their own locality.

In 1941, we of the Pacific Fleet had a plethora of premonitions, of generalized warnings and forebodings that Japan might embark on aggressive action in the Far East at any one of the variously predicted dates. After receipt of such warnings, we were expected to continue with renewed intensity and zeal our own training program and preparations for war rather than to go on an all-out local alert against attack.

In the year 1941 the international situation was grave and, at times, tense. However, preparing the fleet for war through an intensive training program had to go on. There was a vital element of timing involved in determining when the fleet should curtail training for all-out war measures. Maximum security measures, consistent with the maintenance of the training program, were already in effect in the fleet. When would Japanese-American relations reach the point that all training should cease and all-out war dispositions should be made? This was what we needed to know in the Pacific in the year 1941.

The dispatch fixing the hour for the delivery of the Japanese ultimatum to the United States as 1:00 P.M., Washington time, was intercepted and decoded by the Navy Department by 7:00 on the morning of December 7—7:00 A.M., Washington time, 1:30 A.M., Hawaiian time—nearly six and a half hours before the attack. The translation of this short message from the Japanese was a two-minute job. Not later than 9:00 A.M., the Chief of Naval Operations was informed of it. This information was not supplied to me prior to the attack.

I cannot tell from the evidence that has been presented the precise hours on the morning of December 7, when various responsible officers of the Navy Department knew that 1:00 P.M., Washington time, was the hour fixed for the delivery of the Japanese ultimatum to this government. This much I know. There was ample time, at least an interval of approximately three and one-half hours, in which a message could have been dispatched to me. Regardless of what arguments there may be as to the evaluation of the dispatches that had been sent to me, I surely was entitled to know of the hour fixed by Japan for the probable outbreak of war against the United States. I cannot understand now —I have never understood—I may never understand—why I was deprived of the information available in the Navy Department in Washington on Saturday night and Sunday morning.

On November 28, 1941, the Navy Department could have informed me of the following vital facts:

1) Japan had set November 29 as an immovable deadline date for agreement with the United States.

2) The United States gave to Japan certain proposals for a solution of Japanese-American relations on November 26, which amounted to an ultimatum. I might remark parenthetically that an authoritative statement from my government as to the general nature of these proposals would have been most enlightening but it was not supplied.

3) Japan considered the United States proposals of November 26 as unacceptable and planned to rupture negotiations with the United States when her reply to them was delivered to this government.

4) Japan was keeping up a pretext of negotiations after November 26 to conceal a definite plan which went into effect on November 29th.

This was the type of information which I had stated in May I needed so urgently in making the difficult decisions with which I was confronted.

The question will arise in your minds, as it has in mine: Would the receipt of this information have made a difference in the events of December 7? No man can now state as a fact that he would have taken a certain course of action years ago had he known facts which were then unknown to him. All he can give is his present conviction, divorcing himself from hindsight as far as humanly possible, and re-creating the atmosphere of the past and the factors which then influenced him. I give you my views, formed in this manner.

Had I learned these vital facts and the "ships in harbor" messages on *November 28th,* it is my present conviction that I would have rejected the Navy Department's suggestion to send carriers to Wake and Midway. I would have ordered the third carrier, the "Saratoga," back from the West Coast. I would have gone to sea with the fleet and endeavored to keep it in an intercepting position at sea. This would have permitted the disposal of the striking power of the fleet to meet an attack in the Hawaiian area. The requirements of keeping the fleet fueled, however, would have made necessary the presence in Pearl Harbor from time to time of detachments of various units of the main body of the fleet.

On December 4, ample time remained for the Navy Department to forward to me the information which I have outlined, and in addition the following significant facts, which the Navy Department learned between November 27 and that date:

1) Japan had informed Hitler that war with the Anglo-Saxon powers would break out sooner than anyone dreamt;

2) Japan had broadcast her winds code signal using the words "east wind rain," meaning war or a rupture of diplomatic relations with the United States.

Assuming that for the first time *on December 5* I had all the important information then available in the Navy Department, it is my present conviction that I would have gone to sea with the fleet, including the carrier "Lexington" and arranged a rendezvous at sea with Halsey's carrier force, and been in a good position to intercept the Japanese attack.

At some time prior to December 6, 1941, the commanders of Hawaii could have been informed of the promise of armed support as detailed by the War Department in London to Air Marshal Brooke Popham in Singapore. This vital information was denied to them.

On December 6, fifteen hours before the attack, ample time still remained for the Navy Department to give me all the significant facts which I have outlined and which were not available to me in Hawaii. In addition, the Navy Department could then have advised me that thirteen parts of the Japanese reply to the American proposals had been received, that the tone and temper of this message indicated a break in diplomatic relations or war with the United States, and that the Japanese reply was to be formally presented to this government at a special hour soon to be fixed. Had I received this information on the *afternoon of December 6*, it is my present conviction that I would have ordered all fleet units in Pearl Harbor to sea, arranged a rendezvous with Halsey's task force returning from Wake, and been ready to intercept the Japanese force by the time fixed for the outbreak of war.

Even on the morning of December 7, four or five hours before the attack, had the Navy Department for the first time seen fit to send me all this significant information, and the additional fact that 1:00 P.M., Washington time, had been fixed for the delivery of the Japanese ultimatum to the United States, my light forces could have moved out of Pearl Harbor, all ships in the harbor would have been at general quarters, and all resources of the fleet in instant readiness to repel an attack.

The Pacific Fleet deserved a fighting chance. It was entitled to receive from the Navy Department the best information available. Such information had been urgently requested. I had been assured that it would be furnished me. We faced our problems in the Pacific confident that such assurance would be faithfully carried out. . . .

Robert A. *Theobald:* THE FINAL SECRET

One of Admiral Kimmel's chief supporters and friends, Admiral Robert A. Theobald, U.S.N., ret., has written a vigorous little book from which the following is taken. He concludes that Kimmel and the Hawaiian Command were purposely not alerted to the threat of attack from Japan.

Review of the American Moves Which Led to the Japanese Attack

OUR Main Deduction is that President Roosevelt forced Japan to war by unrelenting diplomatic-economic pressure, and enticed that country to initiate hostilities with a surprise attack by holding the Pacific Fleet in Hawaiian waters as an invitation to that attack.

The evidence shows how surely the President moved toward war after June, 1940. His conversation with Admiral Richardson in October, 1940, indicated his conviction that it would be impossible without a stunning incident to obtain a declaration of war from Congress.

Despite the conditions of undeclared war which existed in the Atlantic during the latter half of 1941, it had long been clear that Germany did not intend to contribute to the creation of a state of formal war between her and the United States. The Tripartite Treaty of September, 1940, however, supplied the President with the answer. Under that treaty, war with Japan meant war with Germany and Italy.

The highlights of the ever-increasing pressure upon Japan were:

(1) the extension of financial and military aid to China in concert with Great Britain and the Netherlands, which began early in 1941;

(2) the stoppage of Philippine exports to Japan by Executive Order on May 29, 1941;

(3) the freezing of Japanese assets and the interdiction of all trade with Japan by the United States, Great Britain, and the Netherlands on July 25, 1941;

(4) President Roosevelt's very frank statements of policy to Ambassador Nomura in their conference of August 17, 1941;

(5) the termination of the Washington conference by the American note of November 26, 1941, which brought the war to the United States as the President so clearly intended it would.

That the Pearl Harbor attack was in accord with President Roosevelt's plans is attested by the following array of facts:

(1) President Roosevelt and his military and naval advisers were well aware that Japan invariably started her wars with a surprise attack synchronized closely with her delivery of the Declaration of War;

(2) In October, 1940, the President stated that, if war broke out in the Pacific, Japan would commit the overt act which would bring the United States into the war;

(3) The Pacific Fleet, against contrary naval advice, was retained in Hawaii by order of the President for the alleged

Reprinted from *The Final Secret of Pearl Harbor* by Rear Admiral Robert A. Theobald, U.S.N. retired, published 1954, by The Devin-Adair Co., New York, New York. From pages 192–201.

reason that the Fleet, so located, would exert a restrictive effect upon Japanese aggressions in the Far East;

(4) The Fleet in Hawaii was neither powerful enough nor in the necessary strategic position to influence Japan's diplomatic decisions, which could only be accomplished by the stationing of an adequate naval force in Far Eastern waters;

(5) Before that Fleet could operate at any distance from Pearl Harbor, its train (tankers, supply and repair vessels) would have had to be tremendously increased in strength—facts that would not escape the notice of the experienced Japanese spies in Hawaii;

(6) President Roosevelt gave unmistakable evidence, in March, 1941, that he was not greatly concerned with the Pacific Fleet's effects upon Japanese diplomatic decisions, when he authorized the weakening of that Fleet, already inferior to that of Japan, by the detachment of 3 battleships, 1 aircraft carrier, 4 light cruisers, and 18 destroyers for duty in the Atlantic—a movement which would immediately be detected by Japanese espionage in Hawaii and the Panama Canal Zone;

(7) The successful crippling of the Pacific Fleet was the only surprise operation which promised the Japanese Navy sufficiently large results to justify the risk of heavy losses from land-based air attacks if the surprise failed;

(8) Such an operation against the Fleet in Hawaii was attended with far greater chances of success, especially from the surprise standpoint, and far less risk of heavy losses than a similar attack against that Fleet based in U.S. West Coast ports;

(9) The retention of the Fleet in Hawaii, especially after its reduction in strength in March, 1941, could serve only one possible purpose, an invitation to a surprise Japanese attack;

(10) The denial to the Hawaiian Commanders of all knowledge of Magic was vital to the plan for enticing Japan to deliver a surprise attack upon the Fleet in Pearl Harbor, because, as late as Saturday, December 6, Admiral Kimmel could have caused that attack to be cancelled by taking his Fleet to sea and disappearing beyond land-base human ken.

Review of the Situation Known to Washington Before the Attack

From the beginning of the Washington conference in November, 1941, President Roosevelt and his advisers had repeated evidence that this was Japan's last and supreme effort to break the economic encirclement by peaceful means.

Throughout the negotiations, the Japanese secret dispatches stressed a "deadline date," after which "things were automatically going to happen."

Automatic events which were to follow the breakdown of such vital negotiations could only be acts of war, clear evidence that Japan intended to deliver a surprise attack to initiate the hostilities.

The fact that surprise was essential to the Japanese plans was repeatedly emphasized, on and after November 28, by the Tokyo dispatches and by telephone instructions to the two Ambassadors, cautioning them to keep alive the appearance of continuing negotiation.

Everyone familiar with Japanese military history knew that her first acts of war against China in 1894 and Russia in 1904 had been surprise attacks against the main fleets of those countries.

The only American Naval Force in the Pacific that was worth the risk of such an operation was the Fleet in Hawaiian waters.

The President and his military and

naval advisers well knew, on October 9, from the Tokyo dispatch to Honolulu of September 24, that Japan intended to plan a surprise air attack on the American Fleet in Pearl Harbor, and had daily evidence from the late decodes of certain Tokyo-Honolulu dispatches during the period, December 3–6 inclusive, that the planned attack was soon to occur.

On November 26, the recipients of Magic all had positive information from the Tokyo dispatch to Hong Kong of November 14 that Japan intended war with the United States and Great Britain if the Washington negotiations should fail.

The Tokyo dispatch to the Washington Embassy of November 28 definitely stated that the Japanese Government considered that the American note of the 26th had terminated all possibility of further negotiations.

The Tokyo-Berlin messages dated November 30 instructed the Japanese Ambassador to inform Hitler and von Ribbentrop that war between Japan and the Anglo-Saxon nations would come sooner than anyone expected.

The Japanese code-destruction messages of December 1 and 2 meant that war was extremely close at hand.

With the distribution of the Pilot Message at 3:00 P.M. on Saturday, December 6, the picture was complete for President Roosevelt and the other recipients of Magic, both in Washington and Manila. It said that the answer to the American note was about to arrive in the Embassy, that it was very lengthy, and that its delivery to the U.S. Government was to be especially timed. That timed delivery could only have meant that the answer was a Declaration of War, synchronized with a surprise attack. No other deduction was tenable.

The Saturday receipt of this definite information strongly supported the existing estimates in the War and Navy Departments, that the Japanese surprise attack would be delivered on a Sunday, and marked the morrow, Sunday, December 7, as the day. All this, beyond doubt, was known to President Roosevelt, General Marshall, and Admiral Stark at about 3:00 P.M. on that Saturday, Washington time, 21 hours before the next sunrise in Hawaii.

In obedience to the basic dictates of the Military Art, the information contained in the Pilot Message and the unmistakable implications thereof should have been transmitted to Admiral Kimmel and General Short at once. There was no military consideration that would warrant or tolerate an instant's delay in getting this word to those officers. There cannot be the slightest doubt that General Marshall and Admiral Stark would have had this done, if they had not been restrained from doing so by the orders of President Roosevelt. In the situation which then existed for them, no officer of even limited experience, if free to act, could possibly decide otherwise.

The fighting words in the selected passages of the 13-part message received on that same Saturday were merely additional evidence that this was a Declaration of War. The 14th part received early Sunday morning was further confirmation of that fact.

The 1:00 P.M. Washington delivery, ordered by the time-of-delivery dispatch, clearly indicated Pearl Harbor as the objective of the surprise attack, the final link in the long chain of evidence to that effect.

There Would Have Been No Pearl Harbor If Magic Had Not Been Denied to the Hawaiian Commanders

The recurrent fact of the true Pearl

Harbor story has been the repeated with-holding of information from Admiral Kimmel and General Short. If the War and Navy Departments had been free to follow the dictates of the Art of War, the following is the minimum of informa-tion and orders those officers would have received:

The Tokyo-Honolulu dispatches re-garding the exact berthing of U.S. ships in Pearl Harbor and, in that connection, a reminder that Japan invariably started her wars with a surprise attack on the new enemy's Main Fleet; the dispatches concerning the Washington Conference and the deadline date after which things were automatically going to happen—evidence that this was Japan's last effort to solve U.S.-Japanese differences by peaceful means and the strong intima-tion of the surprise attack; the Tokyo-Hong Kong dispatch of November 14, which told of Japan's intentions to initi-ate war with the two Anglo-Saxon pow-ers if the Washington negotiations failed; the Tokyo-Washington dispatch of No-vember 28, which stated that the Ameri-can note of November 26 had terminated those negotiations; the Pilot Message of December 6, which told that the Decla-ration of War was about to arrive in Washington, and that its delivery to the U.S. Government was to be especially timed, an essential feature for synchron-izing the surprise attack with that de-livery.

Not later than by November 28, the War and Navy Departments should have ordered the Hawaiian Commanders to place the Joint Army-Navy Coastal Frontier Defense Plans in effect, and to unify their Commands; the Navy De-partment should have ordered the mo-bilization of the Naval Establishment.

On November 28, the Chief of Naval Operations should have ordered Admiral Kimmel to recall the *Enterprise* from the Wake operation, and a few days later should have directed the cancellation of the contemplated sending of the *Lexing-ton* to Midway.

As has been repeatedly said, not one word of this information and none of the foregoing orders were sent to Hawaii.

General Marshall Looks Ahead, But Admiral Stark Lets the Cat Out of the Bag

Everything that happened in Wash-ington on Saturday and Sunday, Decem-ber 6 and 7, supports the belief that President Roosevelt had directed that no message be sent to the Hawaiian Commanders before noon on Sunday, Washington time.

General Marshall apparently appre-ciated that failure to act on the Declara-tion of War message and its timed de-livery was going to be very difficult to explain on the witness stand when the future inevitable investigation into the incidents of those days took place. His avoidance of contact with the messages after the Pilot message until 11:25 on Sunday morning was unquestionably prompted by these thoughts. Otherwise, he would undoubtedly have been in his office by 8:00 A.M. on that fateful day.

Admiral Stark, on the other hand, did arrive in his office at 9:25 A.M. on Sun-day, and at once accepted delivery of the full Declaration of War message. Against the advice of his assistants, he refused to inform Admiral Kimmel of its receipt. Forty minutes later, he knew that the 14-part message was to be de-livered to the U.S. Government at 1:00 P.M., Washington time, which was 7:30 A.M., Hawaiian time, as was pointed out to him at once. Again, despite the urging of certain of his aides, he refused to send word to Admiral Kimmel.

Never before in recorded history had a field commander been denied information that his country would be at war in a matter of hours, and that everything pointed to a surprise attack upon his forces shortly after sunrise. No Naval Officer, on his own initiative, would ever make such a decision as Admiral Stark thus did.

That fact and Admiral Stark's decisions on that Sunday morning, even if they had not been supported by the wealth of earlier evidence, would reveal, beyond question, the basic truth of the Pearl Harbor story, namely that these Sunday messages and so many earlier ones, of vital import to Admiral Kimmel's exercise of his command, were not sent because Admiral Stark had orders from the President, which prohibited that action.

This deduction is fully supported by the Admiral's statement to the press in August, 1945, that all he did during the pre-Pearl Harbor days was done on order of higher authority, which can only mean President Roosevelt. The most arresting thing he did, during that time, was to withhold information from Admiral Kimmel.

Roberta Wohlstetter: SIGNALS AND NOISE: THE INTELLIGENCE PICTURE

Mrs. Wohlstetter analyzes the information available on the eve of the Pearl Harbor attack from the standpoint of an intelligence expert and argues that evidence which appears clearcut in hindsight to critics of the Administration did by no means lead to such obvious conclusions for those who had to evaluate it at the time. This selection is the summary from her recent Pearl Harbor: Warning and Decision, *a detailed and careful survey of the problems of intelligence and defense in the months before war came.*

IF our intelligence system and all our other channels of information failed to produce an accurate image of Japanese intentions and capabilities, it was not for want of the relevant materials. Never before have we had so complete an intelligence picture of the enemy. And perhaps never again will we have such a magnificent collection of sources at our disposal.

Retrospect

To review these sources briefly, an American cryptanalyst, Col. William F. Friedman, had broken the top-priority Japanese diplomatic code, which enabled us to listen to a large proportion of the privileged communications between Tokyo and the major Japanese embassies throughout the world. Not only did we know in advance how the

Japanese ambassadors in Washington were advised, and how much they were instructed to say, but we also were listening to top-secret messages on the Tokyo-Berlin and Tokyo-Rome circuits, which gave us information vital for conduct of the war in the Atlantic and Europe. In the Far East this source provided minute details on movements connected with the Japanese program of expansion into Southeast Asia.

Besides the strictly diplomatic codes, our cryptanalysts also had some success in reading codes used by Japanese agents in major American and foreign ports. Those who were on the distribution list for MAGIC had access to much of what these agents were reporting to Tokyo and what Tokyo was demanding of them in the Panama Canal Zone, in cities along the east and west coasts of the Americas from northern Canada as far south as Brazil, and in ports throughout the Far East, including the Philippines and the Hawaiian Islands. They could determine what installations, what troop and ship movements, and what alert and defense measures were of interest to Tokyo at these points on the globe, as well as approximately how much correct information her agents were sending her.

Our naval leaders also had at their disposal the results of radio traffic analysis. While before the war our naval radio experts could not read the content of any Japanese naval or military coded messages, they were able to deduce from a study of intercepted ship call signs the composition and location of the Japanese Fleet units. After a change in call signs, they might lose sight of some units, and units that went into port in home waters were also lost because the ships in port used frequencies that our radios were unable to intercept. Most of the time, however, our traffic analysts had the

various Japanese Fleet units accurately pinpointed on our naval maps.

Extremely competent on-the-spot economic and political analysis was furnished by Ambassador Grew and his staff in Tokyo. Ambassador Grew was himself a most sensitive and accurate observer, as evidenced by his dispatches to the State Department. His observations were supported and supplemented with military detail by frequent reports from American naval attachés and observers in key Far Eastern ports. Navy Intelligence had men with radio equipment located along the coast of China, for example, who reported the convoy movements toward Indochina. There were also naval observers stationed in various high-tension areas in Thailand and Indochina who could fill in the local outlines of Japanese political intrigue and military planning. In Tokyo and other Japanese cities, it is true, Japanese censorship grew more and more rigid during 1941, until Ambassador Grew felt it necessary to disclaim any responsibility for noting or reporting overt military evidence of an imminent outbreak of war. This careful Japanese censorship naturally cut down visual confirmation of the decoded information but very probably never achieved the opaqueness of Russia's Iron Curtain.

During this period the data and interpretations of British intelligence were also available to American officers in Washington and the Far East, though the British and Americans tended to distrust each other's privileged information.

In addition to secret sources, there were some excellent public ones. Foreign correspondents for *The New York Times, The Herald Tribune,* and *The Washington Post* were stationed in Tokyo and Shanghai and in Canberra, Australia.

Their reporting as well as their predictions on the Japanese political scene were on a very high level. Frequently their access to news was more rapid and their judgment of its significance as reliable as that of our Intelligence officers. This was certainly the case for 1940 and most of 1941. For the last few weeks before the Pearl Harbor strike, however, the public newspaper accounts were not very useful. It was necessary to have secret information in order to know what was happening. Both Tokyo and Washington exercised very tight control over leaks during this crucial period, and the newsmen accordingly had to limit their accounts to speculation and notices of diplomatic meetings with no exact indication of the content of the diplomatic exchanges.

The Japanese press was another important public source. During 1941 it proclaimed with increasing shrillness the Japanese government's determination to pursue its program of expansion into Southeast Asia and the desire of the military to clear the Far East of British and American colonial exploitation. This particular source was rife with explicit signals of aggressive intent.

Finally, an essential part of the intelligence picture for 1941 was both public and privileged information on American policy and activities in the Far East. During the year the pattern of action and interaction between the Japanese and American governments grew more and more complex. At the last, it became especially important for anyone charged with the responsibility of ordering an alert to know what moves the American government was going to make with respect to Japan, as well as to try to guess what Japan's next move would be, since Japan's next move would respond in part to ours. Unfortunately our military leaders, and especially our Intelligence officers, were sometimes as surprised as the Japanese at the moves of the White House and the State Department. They usually had more orderly anticipations about Japanese policy and conduct than they had about America's. On the other hand, it was also true that State Department and White House officials were handicapped in judging Japanese intentions and estimates of risk by an inadequate picture of our own military vulnerability.

All of the public and private sources of information mentioned were available to America's political and military leaders in 1941. It is only fair to remark, however, that no single person or agency ever had at any given moment all the signals existing in this vast information network. The signals lay scattered in a number of different agencies; some were decoded, some were not; some traveled through rapid channels of communication, some were blocked by technical or procedural delays; some never reached a center of decision. But it is legitimate to review again the general sort of picture that emerged during the first week of December from the signals readily at hand. Anyone close to President Roosevelt was likely to have before him the following significant fragments.

There was first of all a picture of gathering troop and ship movements down the China coast and into Indochina. The large dimensions of this movement to the south were established publicly and visually as well as by analysis of ship call signs. Two changes in Japanese naval call signs—one on November 1 and another on December 1—had also been evaluated by Naval Intelligence as extremely unusual and as signs of major preparations for some sort of Japanese offensive. The two changes had interfered with the speed of American radio traffic analysis. Thousands of interceptions after December 1 were necessary before the new call signs could be read. Partly for this reason American radio analysts disagreed about the locations of the Japanese carriers. One group held that all the carriers were near Japan because they had not been able to identify a carrier call sign since the middle of November. Another group believed that they had located one carrier division in the Marshalls. The probability seemed to be that the carriers, wherever they were, had gone into radio silence; and past experience led the analysts to believe that they were therefore in waters near the Japanese homeland, where they could communicate with each other on wavelengths that we could not intercept. However, our inability to locate the carriers exactly, combined with the two changes in call signs, was itself a danger signal.

Our best secret source, MAGIC, was confirming the aggressive intention of the new military cabinet in Tokyo, which had replaced the last moderate cabinet on October 17. In particular, MAGIC provided details of some of the preparations for the move into Southeast Asia. Running counter to this were increased troop shipments to the Manchurian border in October. (The intelligence picture is never clear-cut.) But withdrawals had begun toward the end of that month. MAGIC also carried explicit instructions to the Japanese ambassadors in Washington to pursue diplomatic negotiations with the United States with increasing energy, but at the same time it announced a deadline for the favorable conclusion of the negotiations, first for November 25, later postponed until November 29. In case of diplomatic failure by that date, the Japanese ambassadors

were told, Japanese patience would be exhausted, Japan was determined to pursue her Greater East Asia policy, and on November 29 "things" would automatically begin to happen.

On November 26 Secretary Hull rejected Japan's latest bid for American approval of her policies in China and Indochina. MAGIC had repeatedly characterized this Japanese overture as the "last," and it now revealed the ambassadors' reaction of consternation and despair over the American refusal and also their country's characterization of the American Ten Point Note as an "ultimatum."

On the basis of this collection of signals, Army and Navy Intelligence experts in Washington tentatively placed D-day *for the Japanese South-eastern campaign* during the week end of November 30, and when this failed to materialize, during the week end of December 7. They also compiled an accurate list of probable British and Dutch targets and included the Philippines and Guam as possible American targets.

Also available in this mass of information, but long forgotten, was a rumor reported by Ambassador Grew in January, 1941. It came from what was regarded as a not-very-reliable source, the Peruvian embassy, and stated that the Japanese were preparing a surprise air attack on Pearl Harbor. Curiously the date of the report is coincident roughly with what we now know to have been the date of inception of Yamamoto's plan; but the rumor was labeled by everyone, including Ambassador Grew, as quite fantastic and the plan as absurdly impossible. American judgment was consistent with Japanese judgment at this time, since Yamamoto's plan was in direct contradiction to Japanese naval tactical doctrine.

Perspective

On the basis of this rapid recapitulation of the highlights in the signal picture, it is apparent that our decision-makers had at hand an impressive amount of information on the enemy. They did not have the complete list of targets, since none of the last-minute estimates included Pearl Harbor. They did not know the exact hour and date for opening the attack. They did not have an accurate knowledge of Japanese capabilities or of Japanese ability to accept very high risks. The crucial question then, we repeat, is, If we could enumerate accurately the British and Dutch targets and give credence to a Japanese attack against them either on November 30 or December 7, why were we not expecting a specific danger to *ourselves?* And by the word "expecting," we mean expecting in the sense of taking specific alert actions to meet the contingencies of attack by land, sea, or air.

There are several answers to this question that have become apparent in the course of this study. First of all, it is much easier *after* the event to sort the relevant from the irrelevant signals. After the event, of course, a signal is always crystal clear; we can now see what disaster it was signaling, since the disaster has occurred. But before the event it is obscure and pregnant with conflicting meanings. It comes to the observer embedded in an atmosphere of "noise," i.e., in the company of all sorts of information that is useless and irrelevant for predicting the particular disaster. For example, in Washington, Pearl Harbor signals were competing with a vast number of signals from the European theater. These European signals announced danger more frequently and more specifically than any coming from the Far East. The Far Eastern signals were also arriving at a center of decision where they had to compete with the prevailing belief that an unprotected offensive force acts as a deterrent rather than a target. In Honolulu they were competing *not* with signals from the European theater, but rather with a large number of signals announcing Japanese intentions and preparations to attack Soviet Russia rather than to move southward; here they were also competing with expectations of local sabotage prepared by previous alert situations.

In short, we failed to anticipate Pearl Harbor not for want of the relevant materials, but because of a plethora of irrelevant ones. Much of the appearance of wanton neglect that emerged in various investigations of the disaster resulted from the unconscious suppression of vast congeries of signs pointing in every direction except Pearl Harbor. It was difficult later to recall these signs since they had led nowhere. Signals that are characterized today as absolutely unequivocal warnings of surprise air attack on Pearl Harbor become, on analysis in the context of December, 1941, not merely ambiguous but occasionally inconsistent with such an attack. To recall one of the most controversial and publicized examples, the winds code, both General Short and Admiral Kimmel testified that if they had had this information, they would have been prepared on the morning of December 7 for an air attack from without. The messages establishing the winds code are often described in the Pearl Harbor literature as Tokyo's declaration of war against America. If they indeed amounted to such a declaration, obviously the failure to inform Honolulu of this vital news would have been criminal negligence. On examination, however, the messages proved to be instructions for code communication after normal commercial channels had been cut. In one message the recipient was instructed on receipt of an execute to destroy all remaining codes in his possession. In another version the recipient was warned that the execute would be sent out "when relations are becoming dangerous" between Japan and three other countries. There was a different code term for each country: England, America, and the Soviet Union.

There is no evidence that an authentic execute of either message was ever intercepted by the United States before December 7. The message ordering code destruction was in any case superseded by a much more explicit code-destruction order from Tokyo that was intercepted on December 2 and translated on December 3. After December 2, the receipt of a winds-code execute for code destruction would therefore have added nothing new to our information, and code destruction in itself cannot be taken as an unambiguous substitute for a formal declaration of war. During the first week of December the United States ordered all American consulates in the Far East to destroy all American codes, yet no one has attempted to prove that this order was equivalent to an American declaration of war against Japan. As for the other winds-code message, provided an execute had been received warning that relations were dangerous between Japan and the United States, there would still have been no way on the basis of this signal alone to determine whether Tokyo was signaling Japanese intent to attack the United States, or Japanese fear of an American surprise attack (in reprisal for Japanese aggressive moves against American allies in the Far East). It was only after the event that "dangerous relations" could be interpreted as

"surprise air attack on Pearl Harbor."

There is a difference, then, between having a signal available somewhere in the heap of irrelevancies, and perceiving it as a warning; and there is also a difference between perceiving it as a warning, and acting or getting action on it. These distinctions, simple as they are, illuminate the obscurity shrouding this moment in history.

Many instances of these distinctions have been examined in the course of this study. We shall recall a few of the most dramatic now. To illustrate the difference between having and perceiving a signal, let us return to Colonel Fielder, whom we met in Chapter 1. Though he was an untrained and inexperienced Intelligence officer, he headed Army Intelligence at Pearl Harbor at the time of the attack. He had been on the job for only four months, and he regarded as quite satisfactory his sources of information and his contacts with the Navy locally and with Army Intelligence in Washington. Evidently he was unaware that Army Intelligence in Washington was not allowed to send him any "action" or policy information, and he was therefore not especially concerned about trying to read beyond the obvious meaning of any given communication that came under his eyes. Colonel Bratton, head of Army Far Eastern Intelligence in Washington, however, had a somewhat more realistic view of the extent of Colonel Fielder's knowledge. At the end of November, Colonel Bratton had learned about the winds-code setup and was also apprised that the naval traffic analysis unit under Commander Rochefort in Honolulu was monitoring 24 hours a day for an execute. He was understandably worried about the lack of communication between this unit and

Colonel Fielder's office, and by December 5 he finally felt that the matter was urgent enough to warrant sending a message directly to Colonel Fielder about the winds code. Now any information on the winds code, since it belonged to the highest classification of secret information, and since it was therefore automatically evaluated as "action" information, could not be sent through normal G-2 channels. Colonel Bratton had to figure out another way to get the information to Colonel Fielder. He sent this message: "Contact Commander Rochefort immediately thru Commandant Fourteenth Naval District regarding broadcasts from Tokyo reference weather." Signal Corps records establish that Colonel Fielder received this message. How did he react to it? He filed it. According to his testimony in 1945, it made no impression on him and he did not attempt to see Rochefort. He could not sense any urgency behind the lines because he was not expecting immediate trouble, and his expectations determined what he read. A warning signal was available to him, but he did not perceive it.

Colonel Fielder's lack of experience may make this example seem to be an exception. So let us recall the performance of Captain Wilkinson, the naval officer who headed the Office of Naval Intelligence in Washington in the fall of 1941 and who is unanimously acclaimed for a distinguished and brilliant career. His treatment of a now-famous Pearl Harbor signal does not sound much different in the telling. After the event, the signal in question was labeled "the bomb-plot message." It originated in Tokyo on September 24 and was sent to an agent in Honolulu. It requested the agent to divide Pearl Harbor into five areas and to make his future reports on ships in harbor with reference to those areas. Tokyo was especially interested in the locations of battleships, destroyers, and carriers, and also in any information on the anchoring of more than one ship at a single dock.

This message was decoded and translated on October 9 and shortly thereafter distributed to Army, Navy, and State Department recipients of MAGIC. Commander Kramer, a naval expert on MAGIC, had marked the message with an asterisk, signifying that he thought it to be of particular interest. But what was its interest? Both he and Wilkinson agreed that it illustrated the "nicety" of Japanese intelligence, the incredible zeal and efficiency with which they collected detail. The division into areas was interpreted as a device for shortening the reports. Admiral Stark was similarly impressed with Japanese efficiency, and no one felt it necessary to forward the message to Admiral Kimmel. No one read into it a specific danger to ships anchored in Pearl Harbor. At the time, this was a reasonable estimate, since somewhat similar requests for information were going to Japanese agents in Panama, Vancouver, Portland, San Diego, San Francisco, and other places. It should be observed, however, that the estimate was reasonable only on the basis of a very rough check on the quantity of espionage messages passing between Tokyo and these American ports. No one in Far Eastern Intelligence had subjected the messages to any more refined analysis. An observer assigned to such a job would have been able to record an increase in the frequency and specificity of Tokyo's requests concerning Manila and Pearl Harbor in the last weeks before the outbreak of war, and he would have noted that Tokyo was not displaying the same interest in other American ports. These observations, while not significant in isolation, might have been useful in the general signal picture.

There is no need, however, to confine our examples to Intelligence personnel. Indeed, the crucial areas where the signals failed to communicate a warning were in the operational branches of the armed services. Let us take Admiral Kimmel and his reaction to the information that the Japanese were destroying most of their codes in major Far Eastern consulates and also in London and Washington. Since the Pearl Harbor attack, this information has frequently been characterized by military experts who were not stationed in Honolulu as an "unmistakable tip-off." As Admiral Ingersoll explained at the congressional hearings with the lucidity characteristic of statements after the event:

If you rupture diplomatic negotiations you do not necessarily have to burn your codes. The diplomats go home and they can pack up their codes with their dolls and take them home. Also, when you rupture diplomatic negotiations, you do not rupture consular relations. The consuls stay on. Now, in this particular set of dispatches that did not mean a rupture of diplomatic negotiations, it meant war, and that information was sent out to the fleets as soon as we got it. . . .[1]

The phrase "it meant war" was, of course, pretty vague; war in Manila, Hong Kong, Singapore, and Batavia is not war 5000 miles away in Pearl Harbor. Before the event, for Admiral Kimmel, code burning in major Japanese consulates in the Far East may have "meant war," but it did not signal danger of an air attack on Pearl Harbor. In the first place, the information that he received

[1] *Hearings,* Part 9, p. 4226.

was not the original MAGIC. He learned from Washington that Japanese consulates were burning "almost all" of their codes, not all of them, and Honolulu was not included on the list. He knew from a local source that the Japanese consulate in Honolulu was burning secret papers (not necessarily codes), and this back yard burning had happened three or four times during the year. In July, 1941, Kimmel had been informed that the Japanese consulates in lands neighboring Indochina had destroyed codes, and he interpreted the code burning in December as a similar attempt to protect codes in case the Americans or their British and Dutch allies tried to seize the consulates in reprisal for the southern advance. This also was a reasonable interpretation at the time, though not an especially keen one.

Indeed, at the time there was a good deal of evidence available to support all the wrong interpretations of last-minute signals, and the interpretations appeared wrong only *after* the event. There was, for example, a good deal of evidence to support the hypothesis that Japan would attack the Soviet Union from the east while the Russian Army was heavily engaged in the west. Admiral Turner, head of Navy War Plans in Washington, was an enthusiastic adherent of this view and argued the high probability of a Japanese attack on Russia up until the last week in November, when he had to concede that most of Japan's men and supplies were moving south. Richard Sorge, the expert Soviet spy who had direct access to the Japanese Cabinet, had correctly predicted the southern move as early as July, 1941, but even he was deeply alarmed during September and early October by the large number of troop movements to the Manchurian border. He feared that his July advice to the

Soviet Union had been in error, and his alarm ultimately led to his capture on October 14. For at this time he increased his radio messages to Moscow to the point where it was possible for the Japanese police to pinpoint the source of the broadcasts.

It is important to emphasize here that most of the men that we have cited in our examples, such as Captain Wilkinson and Admirals Turner and Kimmel—these men and their colleagues who were involved in the Pearl Harbor disaster—were as efficient and loyal a group of men as one could find. Some of them were exceptionally able and dedicated. The fact of surprise at Pearl Harbor has never been persuasively explained by accusing the participants, individually or in groups, of conspiracy or negligence or stupidity. What these examples illustrate is rather the very human tendency to pay attention to the signals that support current expectations about enemy behavior. If no one is listening for signals of an attack against a highly improbable target, then it is very difficult for the signals to be heard.

For every signal that came into the information net in 1941 there were usually several plausible alternative explanations, and it is not surprising that our observers and analysts were inclined to select the explanations that fitted the popular hypotheses. They sometimes set down new contradictory evidence side by side with existing hypotheses, and they also sometimes held two contradictory beliefs at the same time. We have seen this happen in G-2 estimates for the fall of 1941. Apparently human beings have a stubborn attachment to old beliefs and an equally stubborn resistance to new material that will upset them.

Besides the tendency to select whatever was in accord with one's expecta-tions, there were many other blocks to perception that prevented our analysts from making the correct interpretation. We have just mentioned the masses of conflicting evidence that supported alternative and equally reasonable hypotheses. This is the phenomenon of noise in which a signal is embedded. Even at its normal level, noise presents problems in distraction; but in addition to the natural clatter of useless information and competing signals, in 1941 a number of factors combined to raise the usual noise level. First of all, it had been raised, especially in Honolulu, by the background of previous alert situations and false alarms. Earlier alerts, as we have seen, had centered attention on local sabotage and on signals supporting the hypothesis of a probable Japanese attack on Russia. Second, in both Honolulu and Washington, individual reactions to danger had been numbed, or at least dulled, by the continuous international tension.

A third factor that served to increase the natural noise level was the positive effort made by the enemy to keep the relevant signals quiet. The Japanese security system was an important and successful block to perception. It was able to keep the strictest cloak of secrecy around the Pearl Harbor attack and to limit knowledge only to those closely associated with the details of military and naval planning. In the Japanese Cabinet only the Navy Minister and the Army Minister (who was also Prime Minister) knew of the plan before the task force left its final port of departure.

In addition to keeping certain signals quiet, the enemy tried to create noise, and sent false signals into our information system by carrying on elaborate "spoofs." False radio traffic made us believe that certain ships were maneuvering near the mainland of Japan. The Japanese also sent to individual commanders false war plans for Chinese targets, which were changed only at the last moment to bring them into line with the Southeastern movement.

A fifth barrier to accurate perception was the fact that the relevant signals were subject to change, often very sudden change. This was true even of the so-called static intelligence, which included data on capabilities and the composition of military forces. In the case of our 1941 estimates of the infeasibility of torpedo attacks in the shallow waters of Pearl Harbor, or the underestimation of the range and performance of the Japanese Zero, the changes happened too quickly to appear in an intelligence estimate.

Sixth, our own security system sometimes prevented the communication of signals. It confronted our officers with the problem of trying to keep information from the enemy without keeping it from each other, and, as in the case of MAGIC, they were not always successful. As we have seen, only a very few key individuals saw these secret messages, and they saw them only briefly. They had no opportunity or time to make a critical review of the material, and each one assumed that others who had seen it would arrive at identical interpretations. Exactly who those "others" were was not quite clear to any recipient. Admiral Stark, for example, thought Admiral Kimmel was reading all of MAGIC. Those who were not on the list of recipients, but who had learned somehow of the existence of the decodes, were sure that they contained military as well as diplomatic information and believed that the contents were much fuller and more precise than they actually were. The effect of carefully limiting the reading and discussion of MAGIC, which was certainly

necessary to safeguard the secret of our knowledge of the code, was thus to reduce this group of signals to the point where they were scarcely heard.

To these barriers of noise and security we must add the fact that the necessarily precarious character of intelligence information and predictions was reflected in the wording of instructions to take action. The warning messages were somewhat vague and ambiguous. Enemy moves are often subject to reversal on short notice, and this was true for the Japanese. They had plans for canceling their attacks on American possessions in the Pacific up to 24 hours before the time set for attack. A full alert in the Hawaiian Islands, for example, was one condition that might have caused the Pearl Harbor task force to return to Japan on December 5 or 6. The fact that intelligence predictions must be based on moves that are almost always reversible makes understandable the reluctance of the intelligence analyst to make bold assertions. Even if he is willing to risk his reputation on a firm prediction of attack at a definite time and place, no commander will in turn lightly risk the penalties and costs of a full alert. In December, 1941, a full alert required shooting down any unidentified aircraft sighted over the Hawaiian Islands. Yet this might have been interpreted by Japan as the first overt act. At least that was one consideration that influenced General Short to order his lowest degree of alert. While the cautious phrasing in the messages to the theater is certainly understandable, it nevertheless constituted another block on the road to perception. The sentences in the final theater warnings—"A surprise aggressive move in any direction is a possibility" and "Japanese future action unpredictable but hostile action possible at any moment"—could scarcely have been expected to inform the theater commanders of any change in their strategic situation.

Last but not least we must also mention the blocks to perception and communication inherent in any large bureaucratic organization, and those that stemmed from intraservice and interservice rivalries. The most glaring example of rivalry in the Pearl Harbor case was that between Naval War Plans and Naval Intelligence. A general prejudice against intellectuals and specialists, not confined to the military but unfortunately widely held in America, also made it difficult for intelligence experts to be heard. McCollum, Bratton, Sadtler, and a few others who felt that the signal picture was ominous enough to warrant more urgent warnings had no power to influence decision. The Far Eastern code analysts, for example, were believed to be too immersed in the "Oriental point of view." Low budgets for American Intelligence departments reflected the low prestige of this activity, whereas in England, Germany, and Japan, 1941 budgets reached a height that was regarded by the American Congress as quite beyond reason.

✦ ✦ ✦

In view of all these limitations to perception and communication, is the fact of surprise at Pearl Harbor, then, really so surprising? Even with these limitations explicitly recognized, there remains the step beween perception and action. Let us assume that the first hurdle has been crossed: An available signal has been perceived as an indication of imminent danger. Then how do we resolve the next questions: What specific danger is the signal trying to communicate, and what specific action or preparation should follow?

On November 27, General MacArthur had received a war warning very similar to the one received by General Short in Honolulu. MacArthur's response had been promptly translated into orders designed to protect his bombers from possible air attack from Formosan land bases. But the orders were carried out very slowly. By December 8, Philippine time, only half of the bombers ordered to the south had left the Manila area, and reconnaissance over Formosa had not been undertaken. There was no sense of urgency in preparing for a Japanese air attack, partly because our intelligence estimates had calculated that the Japanese aircraft did not have sufficient range to bomb Manila from Formosa.

The information that Pearl Harbor had been attacked arrived at Manila early in the morning of December 8, giving the Philippine forces some 9 or 10 hours to prepare for an attack. But did an air attack on Pearl Harbor necessarily mean that the Japanese would strike from the air at the Philippines? Did they have enough equipment to mount both air attacks successfully? Would they come from Formosa or from carriers? Intelligence had indicated that they would have to come from carriers, yet the carriers were evidently off Hawaii. MacArthur's headquarters also pointed out that there had been no formal declaration of war against Japan by the United States. Therefore approval could not be granted for a counterattack on Formosan bases. Furthermore there were technical disagreements among airmen as to whether a counterattack should be mounted without advance photographic reconnaissance. While Brereton was arranging permission to undertake photographic reconnaissance, there was further disagreement about what to do with the aircraft in the meantime. Should they be sent aloft or should they be dispersed to avoid destruction in case the Japanese reached the airfields? When the Japanese bombers arrived shortly after noon, they found all the American aircraft wingtip to wingtip on the ground. Even the signal of an actual attack on Pearl Harbor was not an unambiguous signal of an attack on the Philippines, and it did not make clear what response was best.

Samuel Eliot Morison: WHO WAS RESPONSIBLE?

Samuel Eliot Morison, Rear Admiral, U.S.N.R., ret., and professor emeritus of history at Harvard University, has followed his monumental History of United States Naval Operations in World War II *with a concise one-volume work,* The Two-Ocean War, *in which he ranges more freely in discussion of the whys and wherefores. In the selection below, he reviews the question of responsibility, refuting the arguments that Roosevelt knowingly provoked the attack. Morison, author of one of the leading textbooks in American history, along with many other works, has been Harmsworth Professor at Oxford and has won Pulitzer and Bancroft prizes.*

THE Pearl Harbor disaster made a tremendous emotional impact on the American people. The Japanese high command, by their idiotic act, had made a strategic present of the first order to the United States; they had united the country in grim determination to win victory in the Pacific. Isolationism and pacifism now ceased to be valid forces in American politics; but some of their exponents, and many well-meaning people too, became violent propagandists for the bizarre theory that the Roosevelt administration, with the connivance of leading generals and admirals in Washington, knew perfectly well that the attack was coming and deliberately withheld knowledge of it from Kimmel and Short in order, for their own foul purposes, to get us into the war.

Even if one can believe that the late President of the United States was ca-

pable of so horrible a gambit, a little reflection would indicate that he could not possibly have carried it off. He would have needed the connivance of Secretaries Hull, Stimson and Knox, Generals Marshall, Gerow and Miles, Admirals Stark, Turner and Wilkinson, and many of their subordinates, too—all loyal and honorable men who would never have lent themselves to such monstrous deception. More reflection might suggest that if Roosevelt and his cabinet ministers and armed service chiefs had schemed to get us into the war, their purpose would have been better served by warning the Hawaiian commanders in time to get the Fleet to sea and the planes airborne. Even a frustrated attempt to strike Pearl Harbor would have been sufficient *casus belli* to satisfy the most isolationist congressman. Actually, the administration and the heads of the armed forces, as we have seen, were doing their best to prevent or postpone a war with Japan. Roosevelt even sent a personal appeal to Hirohito on the evening of 6 December.

After any overwhelming disaster there is a search for the culprit; and this search is still being pursued, for partisan purposes, after two Navy and two Army investigations and a lengthy congressional one have combed every phase of omission and commission. No military event in our or any other country's history, not even the Battles of Gettysburg and Jutland, has been the subject of such exhaustive research as the air assault on Pearl Harbor.

A principal reason why Washington and Pearl Harbor were caught unawares was their inability to imagine that Japan would do anything so stupid and suicidal. But Joseph Grew in Tokyo—one of the most alert and perceptive ambassadors in United States history—warned Washington on 3 November 1941 against any possible misconception "of the capacity of Japan to rush head-long into a suicidal conflict with the United States. National sanity would dictate against such an event, but Japanese sanity cannot be measured by our own standards of logic. . . . Japan's resort to [war] measures . . . may come with dramatic and dangerous suddenness." Grew's warning fell on deaf ears.

Three weeks later almost everyone in a responsible position in Washington expected Japan to make an aggressive move on the weekend of 29 November; but not on Pearl Harbor. And the curious lethargy into which official Washington seemed to fall after the "war warning" is partly explained by the decrypting of a whole series of dispatches from Tokyo to its ambassadors, to the effect that the deadline was approaching, time was run-

ning out, etc. There were no fewer than 19 such messages between 2 and 26 November, yet nothing had happened.

The Army and Navy cryptographers in Washington were experts, but grossly overworked. The stuff was coming in faster than they could deal with it, and one could not tell which dispatch was important and which was not until all were decrypted.[1] A message from the Japanese consulate at Honolulu dated 6 December, which ended, "There is a considerable opportunity . . . to take advantage for a surprise attack against these places" (Pearl Harbor and vicinity), was not decrypted until after the attack. The "berthing plan" message and Honolulu's replies were not assigned their proper significance at Washington, because they were mixed in with hundreds of messages, which had to be decrypted and translated, from all parts of the world. Observers in China, for instance, were sending as many as fifty messages a week, warning of forthcoming Japanese attacks on Siberia, Peru, and other unlikely places.

Army and Navy Intelligence officers in Washington were somewhat in the position of a woman with a sick child trying to take instructions from a doctor over the telephone while the neighbors are shouting contrary advice in her ear, dogs are barking, children screaming, and trucks roaring by the house. The noise overwhelmed the message. Personalities

[1] In the subsequent "conspiracy" theory of the surprise, much is made of one of the decoding machines being given to the British instead of to Kimmel. It was actually exchanged for machines that the British invented, and Washington wanted, for decrypting certain German ciphers; and since Britain had interests in the Far East at least equal to ours, the exchange was natural and proper. Another machine destined for Pearl Harbor was being constructed when war began. Admiral Hart already had one at Cavite.

also entered into it. Rear Admiral Turner, Navy War Plans officer, was highly opinionated and difficult to work with. He actually forbade the Japanese language officers who did the decrypting and translating, or even the Chief of Naval Intelligence, to make estimates from the dispatches, insisting on doing that himself. And Turner, until late November, was obsessed by the idea that Japan was going to attack Russia, not American or British possessions.

Intelligence data received in Washington were handled in a manner that dissipated their impact. Copies of all decrypted messages that the translators thought significant, sometimes running to 130 a day, were placed in locked briefcases and carried by special messengers to the President, the Secretaries of State, War, and Navy, and about six top-ranking members of the armed forces. The recipient, without taking notes, had to read these signals in the presence of the messenger, who returned them to Army or Navy Intelligence office, where all copies but one were burned. This system, devised for security, denied to all these important people the opportunity to digest data and draw conclusions. It was nobody's particular and exclusive business to study all intelligence material and come up with an estimate. Nobody got anything but excerpts and dribblets.

It must also be remembered that in the late months of 1941 all high Army, Navy and State Department officials in Washington were deeply concerned with the "short of war" conflict in the Atlantic, and with Europe, where it then seemed probable that Hitler would gobble up Russia as he had France, order American merchantmen to be sunk, and step up his subversive activities in Central and South America.

Every one of the Japanese messages decrypted and translated before 7 December was ambiguous. None mentioned Pearl Harbor. None even pointed clearly at Japanese intent to attack the United States anywhere. Thus, no clear warnings were sent to Hawaii because Washington saw no reason to anticipate an attack on Hawaii. Washington, moreover, was determined not to begin a war with Japan. That was the meaning of the passage in the diary of War Secretary Stimson, recording the cabinet meeting of 25 November, after one of Tojo's deadline messages had been decrypted and translated. "The President predicted that we were likely to be attacked perhaps next Monday. . . . The question was how we should maneuver them into the position of firing the first shot." This quotation has been made much of by those trying to prove conspiracy between F.D.R. and his cabinet to get us into war. Mr. Stimson's use of the verb "maneuver" was unfortunate, but his intent is clear—we were not going to provoke the Japanese by an overt act; peace would continue until and unless they chose to strike. This was exactly the same attitude as President Lincoln's about Fort Sumter; or, to go further back, Colonel Parker's classic speech to the Minutemen at Lexington on 19 April 1775: "Don't fire unless fired upon, but if they mean to have a war, let it begin here."

Pearl Harbor, besides lacking the complete Intelligence picture, had the additional handicap of divided responsibility. General Short was charged with the defense of Oahu, including Pearl Harbor and antiaircraft batteries ashore; Admiral Bloch, commandant Fourteenth Naval District, was responsible for the defense of the Navy Yard, and Admiral Kimmel for that of the Fleet. Relations between them were friendly but inadequate; each one, as we have seen, assumed that the others were doing something that they didn't do.

A series of false assumptions, both at Washington and Oahu, added up to something as serious as the sins of omission. In Hawaii, the Navy assumed that the Army had gone on full alert, and that the radar warning net was completely operational. The Army assumed that the Navy was conducting an effective air reconnaissance around the island. Admiral Kimmel assumed that aërial torpedoes could not operate in the shoal waters of Pearl Harbor. Both Army and Navy Intelligence officers assumed that Japan was sending all her naval forces south, and that in any event Japan would not be so stupid as to attack Pearl Harbor. In Washington, Colonel Bratton of Army Intelligence assumed that the Pacific Fleet would go to sea after the 27 November "war warning," so to him the intercepted reports of ships' positions by the Japanese consulate registered waste effort; and Captain Wilkinson of Naval Intelligence assumed that these reports were simply evidence of the Japanese inordinate love for detail. Rear Admiral Turner of War Plans assumed that this and all other relevant intelligence was going to Admiral Kimmel, and General Gerow of Army War Plans assumed that Kimmel and Short were exchanging every scrap of what they did get, which was considerable. Washington was as vague and uncertain about what was going to happen on the first or second weekend after 27 November as Pearl Harbor itself. It was a case of the blind *not* leading the blind; false assumptions at both ends of the line.

The gravest charge against Admiral Kimmel and General Short is that they virtually ignored the "war warning" dispatch of 27 November from Washington. Admiral Kimmel, as we have seen, did send air reinforcement promptly to Wake and Midway Islands. He had already (with Admiral Bloch's coöperation) set up the surface and air patrol off the mouth of Pearl Harbor which encountered the midget submarines. He had, on 14 October, warned the Fleet against a submarine attack as a herald of something worse. Thus, the charge whittles down to this: that he did not repeat this warning and beef-up air patrol after 27 November. He thought that he had done everything that could reasonably be expected, in view of the intelligence received. Nevertheless, an "unwarranted feeling of immunity from attack" prevailed in Oahu at the crucial moment, as Admiral King observed; and it is not unfair to hold Kimmel and Short responsible.

Finally, we have to consider the "East Wind, Rain" dispatch which, by people bent on proving dastardly deception by Washington, has been blown up to a definite word from Tokyo that Pearl Harbor was about to be attacked. Actually, it was nothing of the sort. On 19 November, Tokyo notified the principal Japanese representatives abroad, in a dispatch that Washington decrypted, that if all other means of communication failed, they would be ordered to destroy codes in a plain-language weather broadcast. In this broadcast, "East Wind, Rain" would mean, "Japanese-United States relations in danger"; "North Wind, Cloudy" would mean the same as to Russia; "West Wind, Clear" would mean the same as to England. There was no mention of Pearl Harbor, or any other target; not even a clear forecast of war. This "Winds" message, however, was taken seriously in Washington where a number of officers were alerted to watch Japanese broadcasts for the false weather forecast. Whether or not that was ever sent is disputed; but in no case would it have told Washington or Hawaii anything more than what they already knew, viz., that Japanese embassies had been ordered to destroy their codes.

Fundamentally, however, it was the system, the setup both at Washington and at Pearl, rather than individual stupidity or apathy, which muffled and confused what was going on. No one person knew the whole picture that the intelligence data disclosed; no one person was responsible for the defense of Pearl Harbor; too many people assumed that others were taking precautions that they did not take.

＊　＊　＊

The Japanese war plan, brought together at a Supreme War Council on 6 September 1941, was as follows: First, prior to a declaration of war, destruction of the United States Pacific Fleet and the British and American air forces on the Malay Peninsula and Luzon. Second, while the British and American Navies were decimated and disorganized, a quick conquest of the Philippines, Guam, Wake, Hong Kong, Borneo, British Malaya (including Singapore), and Sumatra. Third, when these were secure, the converging of Japanese amphibious forces on the richest prize, Java, and a mop-up of the rest of the Dutch islands. Fourth, an intensive development of Malayan and Indonesian resources in oil, rubber, etc.; and, to secure these, establishment of a defensive perimeter running from the Kurile Islands through Wake, the Marshalls, and around the southern and western edges of the Malay Barrier to the Burmese-Indian border. With these bases the Japanese Navy and air forces could cut all lines of communication between Australia, New Zealand and the Anglo-American powers, which would then be forced to sue for peace. Fifth and finally, Japan would proceed completely to subjugate China. Over half the world's population would then be under the economic, political and military control of the Emperor.

This scheme of conquest was the most enticing, ambitious and far-reaching in modern history, not excepting Hitler's. It almost worked, and might well have succeeded but for the United States Navy.

This being Japan's plan, it is astonishing to find her American apologists claiming that she was goaded, provoked and coerced into making war on us by the Roosevelt administration. . . .

Paul W. Schroeder: AN APPRAISAL

*In this final selection attention is shifted back from the issue of im-
mediate responsibility for the surprise at Pearl Harbor to the more
general question of United States policy toward Japan. Professor Paul
W. Schroeder, formerly at the University of Texas and now professor
of history at the University of Illinois, believes that a "hard" policy
toward Japan may have been a mistake, as far as America's long-range
advantage was concerned and raises the perplexing question of realism
and morality in foreign affairs in this summary passage from his* The
Axis Allliance and Japanese-American Relations.

In judging American policy toward
Japan in 1941, it might be well to
separate what is still controversial from
what is not. There is no longer any real
doubt that the war came about over
China. Even an administration stalwart
like Henry L. Stimson and a sympathetic
critic like Herbert Feis concur in this.[1]
Nor is it necessary to speculate any
longer as to what could have induced
Japan to launch such an incredible attack upon the United States and Great
Britain as occurred at Pearl Harbor and
in the south Pacific. One need not, as
Winston Churchill did in wartime, char-
acterize it as "an irrational act" incom-
patible "with prudence or even with
sanity."[2] The Japanese were realistic
about their position throughout, they did
not suddenly go insane. The attack was
an act of desperation, not madness. Japan fought only when she had her back
to the wall as a result of America's diplomatic and economic offensive.

The main point still at issue is whether
the United States was wise in maintaining a "hard" program of diplomatic and
economic pressure on Japan from July
1941 on. Along with this issue go two
subsidiary questions: the first, whether it
was wise to make the liberation of China
the central aim of American policy and
the immediate evacuation of Japanese
troops a requirement for agreement; the
second, whether it was wise to decline
Premier Konoye's invitation to a meeting of leaders in the Pacific. On all these
points, the policy which the United
States carried out still has distinguished
defenders. The paramount issue between
Japan and the United States, they con-
tend, always was the China problem. In
her China policy, Japan showed that she
was determined to secure domination
over a large area of East Asia by force.
Apart from the legitimate American
commercial interests which would be
ruined or excluded by this Japanese
action, the United States, for reasons of

[1] "If at any time the United States had been
willing to concede Japan a free hand in China,
there would have been no war in the Pacific"
(Stimson and Bundy, *On Active Service*, 256).
"Our full induction into this last World War
followed our refusal to let China fend for itself.
We had rejected all proposals which would
have allowed Japan to remain in China and
Manchuria. . . . Japan had struck—rather than
accept frustration" (Herbert Feis, *The China
Tangle* [Princeton: Princeton University Press,
1953], 3).
[2] Speech to U.S. Congress, Washington, Dec.
26, 1941, *War Speeches of Churchill*, II, 150.

From *The Axis Alliance and Japanese-American Relations*, pp. 200–216. Copyright, 1958, by the
American Historical Association, used with permission of Cornell University Press.

her own security and of world peace, had sufficient stake in Far Eastern questions to oppose such aggression. Finally, after ten years of Japanese expansion, it was only sensible and prudent for the United States to demand that it come to an end and that Japan retreat. In order to meet the Japanese threat, the United States had a perfect right to use the economic power she possessed in order to compel the Japanese to evacuate their conquered territory. If Japan chose to make this a cause for war, the United States could not be held responsible.

A similar defense is offered on the decision to turn down Konoye's Leaders' Conference. Historians may concede, as do Langer and Gleason, that Konoye was probably sincere in wanting peace and that he "envisaged making additional concessions to Washington, including concessions on the crucial issue of the withdrawal of Japanese troops from China." But, they point out, Konoye could never have carried the Army with him on any such concession.[3] If the United States was right in requiring Japan to abandon the Co-Prosperity Sphere, then her leaders were equally right in declining to meet with a Japanese Premier who, however conciliatory he might have been personally, was bound by his own promises and the exigencies of Japanese politics to maintain this national aim. In addition, there was the serious possibility that much could be lost from such a meeting—the confidence of China, the cohesiveness of the coalition with Great Britain and Russia. In short, there was not enough prospect of gain to merit taking the chance.

This is a point of view which must be taken seriously. Any judgment on the wisdom or folly of the American policy, in fact, must be made with caution—there are no grounds for dogmatic certainty. The opinion here to be developed, nonetheless, is that the American policy from the end of July to December was a grave mistake. It should not be necessary to add that this does not make it treason. There is a "back door to war" theory, espoused in various forms by Charles A. Beard, George Morgenstern, Charles C. Tansill, and, most recently, Rear Admiral Robert A. Theobald, which holds that the President chose the Far East as a rear entrance to the war in Europe and to that end deliberately goaded the Japanese into an attack.[4] This theory is quite different and quite incredible. It is as impossible to accept as the idea that Japan attacked the United States in a spirit of overconfidence or that Hitler pushed the Japanese into war. Roosevelt's fault, if any, was not that of deliberately provoking the Japanese to attack, but of allowing Hull and others to talk him out of impulses and ideas which, had he pursued them, might have averted the conflict. Moreover, the mistake (assuming that it was a mistake) of a too hard and rigid policy with Japan was, as has been pointed out, a mistake shared by the whole nation, with causes that were deeply organic. Behind it was not sinister design or warlike intent, but a sincere and uncompromising adherence to moral principles and liberal doctrines.

This is going ahead too fast, however; one needs first of all to define the mistake with which American policy is

---

[3] Langer and Gleason, *Undeclared War*, 706–707.

[4] Charles A. Beard, *President Roosevelt and the Coming of the War, 1941* (New Haven: Yale University Press, 1948); George E. Morgenstern, *Pearl Harbor: The Story of the Secret War* (New York: Devin-Adair, 1947); Charles C. Tansill, *Back Door to War* (Chicago: Regnery, 1952); Rear Admiral Robert A. Theobald, *The Final Secret of Pearl Harbor* (New York: Devin-Adair, 1954).

charged. Briefly, it was this. In the attempt to gain everything at once, the United States lost her opportunity to secure immediately her essential requirements in the Far East and to continue to work toward her long-range goals. She succeeded instead only in making inevitable an unnecessary and avoidable war—an outcome which constitutes the ultimate failure of diplomacy. Until July 1941, as already demonstrated, the United States consistently sought to attain two limited objectives in the Far East, those of splitting the Axis and of stopping Japan's advance southward. Both aims were in accordance with America's broad strategic interests; both were reasonable, attainable goals. Through a combination of favorable circumstance and forceful American action, the United States reached the position where the achievement of these two goals was within sight. At this very moment, on the verge of a major diplomatic victory, the United States abandoned her original goals and concentrated on a third, the liberation of China. This last aim was not in accord with American strategic interests, was not a limited objective, and, most important, was completely incapable of being achieved by peaceful means and doubtful of attainment even by war. Through her single-minded pursuit of this unattainable goal, the United States forfeited the diplomatic victory which she had already virtually won. The unrelenting application of extreme economic pressure on Japan, instead of compelling the evacuation of China, rendered war inevitable, drove Japan back into the arms of Germany for better or for worse, and precipitated the wholesale plunge by Japan into the South Seas. As it ultimately turned out, the United States succeeded in liberating China only at great cost and when it was too late

to do the cause of the Nationalist Chinese much real good.

This is not, of course, a new viewpoint. It is in the main simply that of Ambassador Grew, who has held and defended it since 1941. The arguments he advances seem cogent and sensible in the light of present knowledge. Briefly summarized, they are the following: First is his insistence on the necessity of distinguishing between long-range and immediate goals in foreign policy and on the folly of demanding the immediate realization of both.[5] Second is his contention that governments are brought to abandon aggressive policies not by sudden conversion through moral lectures, but by the gradual recognition that the policy of aggression will not succeed. According to Grew, enough awareness of failure existed in the government of Japan in late 1941 to enable it to make a beginning in the process of reversal of policy —but not nearly enough to force Japan to a wholesale surrender of her conquests and aims.[6] Third was his conviction that what was needed on both sides was time —time in which the United States could grow stronger and in which the tide of war in Europe could be turned definitely against Germany, time in which the sense of failure could grow in Japan and in which moderates could gain better control of the situation. A victory in Europe, Grew observed, would either automatically solve the problem of Japan or make that problem, if necessary, much easier to solve by force.[7] Fourth was his belief that Japan would fight if backed to the wall (a view vindicated by events)[8] and

---

[5] Grew, *Turbulent Era*, II, 1255.
[6] *Ibid.*, 1290.
[7] *Ibid.*, 1268–1269, 1286.
[8] The opposite belief, that Japan would give way, not only was inconsonant with the best available political and military intelligence, but was also a bad estimate of Japanese national

that a war at this time with Japan could not possibly serve the interests of the United States. Even if one considered war as the only final answer to Japanese militarism, still, Grew would answer, the United States stood to gain nothing by seeking a decision in 1941. The time factor was entirely in America's favor. Japan could not hope to gain as much from a limited relaxation of the embargo as the United States could from time gained for mobilization; Roosevelt and the military strategists were in fact anxious to gain time by a *modus vivendi.*[9]

There is one real weakness in Grew's argument upon which his critics have always seized. This is his contention that Konoye, faced after July 26 with the two clear alternatives of war or a genuine peace move, which would of necessity include a settlement with China, had chosen the latter course and could have carried through a policy of peace had he been given the time. "We believed," he writes, "that Prince Konoye was in a position to carry the country with him in a program of peace" and to make commitments to the United States which would "eventually, if not immediately" meet the conditions of Hull's Four Points.[10] The answer of critics is that, even if one credits Konoye's sincerity and takes his assurances at face value, there is still no reason to believe that he could

have carried even his own cabinet, much less the whole nation, with him on any program approximating that of Hull. In particular, as events show, he could not have persuaded the Army to evacuate China.[11]

The objection is well taken; Grew was undoubtedly over-optimistic about Konoye's capacity to carry through a peaceful policy. This one objection, however, does not ruin Grew's case. He countered it later with the argument that a settlement with Japan which allowed Japanese garrisons to remain in China on a temporary basis would not have been a bad idea. Although far from an ideal solution, it would have been better, for China as well, than the policy the United States actually followed. It would have brought China what was all-important—a cessation of fighting—without involving the United States, as many contended, in either a sacrifice of principle or a betrayal of China. The United States, Grew points out, had never committed herself to guaranteeing China's integrity. Further, it would not have been necessary to agree to anything other than temporary garrisons in North China which, in more favorable times, the United States could work to have removed. The great mistake was to allow American policy to be guided by a sentimental attitude toward China which in the long run could do neither the United States nor China any good. As Grew puts it:

Japan's advance to the south, including her occupation of portions of China, constituted for us a real danger, and it was definitely in our national interest that it be stopped, by peaceful means if possible, by force of arms if necessary. American aid to China should have been regarded, as we believe it was

---

psychology and of expansionist psychology in general. F. C. Jones rightly criticizes it as "the folly of supposing that the rulers of a powerful nation, having committed themselves to an expansionist policy, will abandon or reverse that policy when confronted by the threat of war. So long as they see, or think they see, any possibility of success, they will elect to fight rather than face the humiliation and probable internal revolt which submission to the demands of their opponents would entail" (*Japan's New Order*, 461).

[9] Grew, *Turbulent Era*, II, 1276–1277.
[10] *Ibid.*, 1263–1264.

[11] Feis, *Road to Pearl Harbor*, 275–277; Jones, *Japan's New Order*, 457–458.

regarded by our Government, as an indirect means to this end, and not from a sentimental viewpoint. The President's letter of January 21, 1941, shows that he then sensed the important issues in the Far East, and that he did not include China, purely for China's sake, among them. . . . The failure of the Washington Administration to seize the opportunity presented in August and September, 1941, to halt the southward advance by peaceful means, together with the paramount importance attached to the China question during the conversations in Washington, gives rise to the belief that not our Government but millions of quite understandably sympathetic but almost totally uninformed American citizens had assumed control of our Far Eastern policy.[12]

There remains the obvious objection that Grew's solution, however plausible it may now seem, was politically impracticable in 1941. No American government could then have treated China as expendable, just as no Japanese government could have written off the China Affair as a dead loss. This is in good measure true and goes a long way to explain, if not to justify, the hard American policy. Yet it is not entirely certain that no solution could have been found which would both have averted war and have been accepted by the American people, had a determined effort been made to find one. As F. C. Jones points out, the United States and Japan were not faced in July 1941 with an absolute dilemma of peace or war, of complete settlement or open conflict. Hull believed that they were, of course; but his all-or-nothing attitude constituted one of his major shortcomings as a diplomat. Between the two extremes existed the possibility of a *modus vivendi*, an agreement settling some issues and leaving others in abeyance. Had Roosevelt and

Konoye met, Jones argues, they might have been able to agree on a relaxation of the embargo in exchange for satisfactory assurances on the Tripartite Pact and southward expansion, with the China issue laid aside. The United States would not have had to cease aid, nor Japan to remove her troops. The final settlement of the Far Eastern question, Jones concludes,

would then have depended upon the issue of the struggle in Europe. If Germany prevailed, then the United States would be in no position to oppose Japanese ambitions in Asia; if Germany were defeated, Japan would be in no position to persist in those ambitions in the face of the United States, the USSR, and the British Commonwealth.[13]

Such an agreement, limited and temporary in nature, would have involved no sacrifice of principle for either nation, yet would have removed the immediate danger of war. As a temporary expedient and as an alternative to otherwise inevitable and useless conflict, it could have been sold by determined effort to the public on both sides. Nor would it have been impossible, in the writer's opinion, to have accompanied or followed such an agreement with a simple truce or standstill in the China conflict through American mediation.

This appraisal, to be sure, is one based on realism. Grew's criticism of Hull's policy and the alternative he offers to it are both characterized by fundamental attention to what is practical and expedient at a given time and to limited objectives within the scope of the national interest. In general, the writer agrees with this point of view, believing that, as William A. Orton points out, it is foolish and disastrous to treat nations as morally responsible persons, "because their na-

[12] Grew, *Turbulent Era,* II, 1367–1368.

[13] Jones, *Japan's New Order,* 459.

ture falls far short of personality," and that, as George F. Kennan contends, the right role for moral considerations in foreign affairs is not to determine policy, but rather to soften and ameliorate actions necessarily based on the realities of world politics.[14]

From this realistic standpoint, the policy of the State Department would seem to be open to other criticisms besides those of Grew. The criticisms, which may be briefly mentioned here, are those of inconsistency, blindness to reality, and futility. A notable example of the first would be the inconsistency of a strong no-compromise stand against Japan with the policy of broad accommodation to America's allies, especially Russia, both before and after the American entrance into the war.[15] The inconsistency may perhaps best be seen by comparing the American stand in 1941 on such questions as free trade, the Open Door in China, the territorial and administrative integrity of China, the maintenance of the prewar *status quo* in the Far East, and the sanctity of international agreements with the position taken on the same

[14] William A. Orton, *The Liberal Tradition* (New Haven: Yale University Press, 1944), 239; George F. Kennan, *American Diplomacy, 1900–1950* (Chicago: University of Chicago Press, 1951), 95–103.
[15] One notes with interest, for example, a pre-Pearl Harbor statement by Senator Lister Hill of Alabama, a strong proponent of a radical anti-Japanese policy, as to America's attitude toward the Soviet Union: "It is not the business of this government to ask or to receive any assurance from Stalin about what he will do with regard to Finland after the war. . . . It is the business of this government to look out for and defend the vital interests of the United States" (*New York Times*, Nov. 5, 1941). If in the above quotation one reads "Tojo" for "Stalin" and "China" for "Finland," the result is a statement of the extreme isolationist position on the Far East which Hill and other supporters of the administration found so detestable.

questions at the Yalta Conference in 1945.[16]

[16] The writer has no desire to enter here into the controversy over the merits of the Yalta decisions, but only to draw a certain parallel. The standard defense for the Yalta policy on the Far East has been the contention that the United States conceded to Soviet Russia only what the U.S.S.R. could and would have seized without American leave, that the only alternative to agreement would have been war with Russia, and that securing Russian entrance into the Far Eastern war was considered militarily necessary (George F. Lensen, "Yalta and the Far East," in John L. Snell, Forrest C. Pogue, Charles F. Delzell, and George F. Lensen, *The Meaning of Yalta: Big Three Diplomacy and the New Balance of Power* [Baton Rouge: Louisiana State University Press, 1956], 163–164). The argument may be quite sound, but surely it would serve equally well—indeed, much better, *mutatis mutandis*—to justify a policy of conciliation toward Japan in 1941. Applied to Japan, the argument would then read as follows: The United States would have conceded to Japan only the temporary possession of a part of what Japan had already seized without American leave; the only alternative to agreement would have been war with Japan; and preventing Japanese entrance into the European war was considered militarily necessary. The great difference between the two situations would seem to be that the concessions envisioned by Japan in 1941 were temporary and reversible; those gained by Russia in 1945 were not. The very necessity of pursuing the Yalta policy in 1945 casts doubt on the wisdom of the hard-and-fast stand of 1941. Felix Morley has put the parallel neatly: "To assert that the sudden and complete reversal of the long-established Far Eastern policy was justified was also to say, by implication, that the policy reversed was fundamentally faulty, that to fight a war with Japan in behalf of Chinese nationalism had been a dreadful mistake" (*The Foreign Policy of the United States* [New York: Alfred A. Knopf, 1951], 87–88). One may, as Morley does, reject both the above premise and the conclusion, or one may accept both; but it is difficult to see how one may affirm the premise and deny the conclusion. For those who believe that a vital moral difference existed between the two cases, the problem would seem to be how to show that it is morally unjustifiable to violate principle in order to keep a potential enemy out of a war, yet morally justifiable to sacrifice principle in order to get a potential ally into it. The dilemma appears insoluble.

The blindness to reality may be seen in the apparent inability of American policy makers to take seriously into account the gravity of Japan's economic plight or the real exigencies of her military and strategic position, particularly as these factors would affect the United States over the long run.[17] Equally unrealistic and more fateful was the lack of appreciation on the part of many influential people and of wide sections of the public of the almost certain consequences to be expected from the pressure exerted on Japan—namely, American involvement in a war her military strategists considered highly undesirable. The attitude has been well termed by Robert Osgood, "this blind indifference toward the military and political consequences of a morally-inspired position."[18]

The charge of futility, finally, could be laid to the practice of insisting on a literal subscription to principles which, however noble, had no chance of general acceptance or practical application. The best example is the persistent demand that the Japanese pledge themselves to carrying out nineteenth-century principles of free trade and equal access to raw materials in a twentieth-century world where economic nationalism and autarchy, trade barriers and restrictions were everywhere the order of the day, and not the least in the United States under the New Deal. Not one of America's major allies would have subscribed wholeheartedly to Hull's free-trade formula; what good it could have done to pin the Japanese down to it is hard to determine.[19]

But these are all criticisms based on a realistic point of view, and to judge the American policy solely from this point of view is to judge it unfairly and by a standard inappropriate to it. The policy of the United States was avowedly not one of realism, but of principle. If then it is to be understood on its own grounds and judged by its own standards, the main question will be whether the policy was morally right—that is, in accord with principles of peace and international justice. Here, according to its defenders, the American policy stands vindicated. For any other policy, any settlement with Japan at the expense of China, would have meant a betrayal not only of China, but also of vital principles and of America's moral task in the world.

This, as we know, was the position of Hull and his co-workers. It has been

---

[17] In his very interesting book, *America's Strategy in World Politics* (New York: Harcourt, Brace, 1942), Nicholas Spykman displays some of the insights which seem to have been lacking in the American policy of the time. He points out, for example, that Japan's economic and geographic position was essentially the same as that of Great Britain; that her position vis-à-vis the United States was also roughly equivalent to England's; that therefore it made little sense for America to aid Great Britain in maintaining a European balance of power, while at the same time trying to force Japan to give up all her buffer states in Asia; that the Japanese war potential could not compare to that of a revivified and unified China; and that one day (a striking prediction in 1942!) the United States would have to undertake to protect Japan from Soviet Russia and China (pp. 135–137, 469–470). Spykman saw then what is today so painfully evident—that without a Japanese foothold on the Asiatic mainland no real balance of power is possible in Asia.

[18] Robert E. Osgood, *Ideals and Self-Interest in America's Foreign Relations* (Chicago: University of Chicago Press, 1953), 361.

[19] A memorandum by the Chief of the State Department Division of Commercial Policy and Agreements (Hawkins) to Ballantine, Washington, Nov. 10, 1941, offers interesting comments on the extent and nature of the trade discriminations then being practiced against Japan by nations throughout the world, including the United States (*Foreign Relations, 1941*, IV, 576–577).

stated more recently by Basil Rauch, who writes:

No one but an absolute pacifist would argue that the danger of war is a greater evil than violation of principle. . . . The isolationist believes that appeasement of Japan without China's consent violated no principle worth a risk of war. The internationalist must believe that the principle did justify a risk of war.[20]

This is not an argument to be dismissed lightly. The contention that the United States had a duty to fulfill in 1941, and that this duty consisted in holding to justice and morality in a world given to international lawlessness and barbarism and in standing on principle against an unprincipled and ruthless aggressor, commands respect. It is not answered by dismissing it as unrealistic or by proscribing all moral considerations in foreign policy. An answer may be found, however, in a closer definition of America's moral duty in 1941. According to Hull, and apparently also Rauch, the task was primarily one of upholding principle. This is not the only possible definition. It may well be contended that the moral duty was rather one of doing the most practical good possible in a chaotic world situation and, further, that this was the main task President Roosevelt and the administration had in mind at least till the end of July 1941.

If the moral task of the United States in the Far East was to uphold a principle of absolute moral value, the principle of nonappeasement of aggressors, then the American policy was entirely successful in fulfilling it. The American diplomats proved that the United States was capable of holding to its position in disregard and even in defiance of national interests narrowly conceived. If, however, the task

was one of doing concrete good and giving practical help where needed, especially to China, then the American policy falls fatally short. For it can easily be seen not only that the policy followed did not in practice help China, but also that it could not have been expected to. Although it was a pro-China and even a China-first policy in principle, it was not in practical fact designed to give China the kind of help needed.

What China required above all by late 1941 was clearly an end to the fighting, a chance to recoup her strength. Her chaotic financial condition, a disastrous inflation, civil strife with the Communists, severe hunger and privation, and falling morale all enfeebled and endangered her further resistance. Chiang Kai-shek, who knew this, could hope only for an end to the war through the massive intervention of American forces and the consequent liberation of China. It was in this hope that he pleaded so strongly for a hard American policy toward Japan. Chiang's hopes, however, were wholly unrealistic. For though the United States was willing to risk war for China's sake, and finally did incur it over the China issue, the Washington government never intended in case of war to throw America's full weight against Japan in order to liberate China. The American strategy always was to concentrate on Europe first, fighting a defensive naval war in the Far East and aiding China, as before, in order to keep the Japanese bogged down. The possibility was faced and accepted that the Chinese might have to go on fighting for some years before eventual liberation through the defeat of Japan. The vehement Chinese protests over this policy were unavailing, and the bitter disillusionment suffered by the Chinese only helped to bring on in 1942 the virtual collapse of the Chi-

[20] Rauch, *Roosevelt*, 472.

nese war effort during the latter years of the war.[21]

As a realistic appraisal of America's military capabilities and of her world-wide strategic interests, the Europe-first policy has a great deal to recommend it. But the combination of this realistic strategy with a moralistic diplomacy led to the noteworthy paradox of a war incurred for the sake of China which could not then be fought for the sake of China and whose practical value for China at the time was, to say the least, dubious. The plain fact is that the United States in 1941 was not capable of forcing Japan out of China by means short of war and was neither willing nor, under existing circumstances, able to throw the Japanese out by war. The American government could conceivably have told the Chinese this and tried to work out the best possible program of help for China under these limitations. Instead, it yielded to Chinese importunities and followed a policy almost sure to eventuate in war, knowing that if the Japanese did attack, China and her deliverance would have to take a back seat. It is difficult to conceive of such a policy as a program of practical aid to China.

The main, though not the only, reason why this policy was followed is clearly the overwhelming importance of principle in American diplomacy, particularly the principle of nonappeasement of aggressors. Once most leaders in the administration and wide sections of the public became convinced that it was America's prime moral duty to stand hard and fast against aggressors, whatever the consequences, and once this conviction became decisive in the formulation of policy, the end result was almost inevitable: a policy designed to uphold principle and to punish the aggressor, but not to save the victim.[22]

It is this conviction as to America's moral duty, however sincere and understandable, which the writer believes constitutes a fundamental misreading of America's moral task. The policy it gave rise to was bad not simply because it was moralistic but because it was obsessed with the wrong kind of morality—with that abstract "Let justice be done though the heavens fall" kind which so often, when relentlessly pursued, does more harm than good. It would be interesting to investigate the role which this concep-

[21] Levi, *Modern China's Foreign Policy*, 229–237. On the danger of internal collapse in China as early as 1940, see U.S. Department of State, *Foreign Relations of the United States: 1940*, vol. IV, *The Far East* (Washington: Government Printing Office, 1955), 672–677.

[22] It is Secretary of War Henry L. Stimson who gives evidence on how strong was the role of avenging justice in the prevailing picture of America's moral duty. He displays a striking anxiety to acquit the administration of the charge of being "soft" on Japan and to prove that the administration was always fully aware of the Japanese crimes and morally aroused by them. The nation's leaders, he insists in one place, were "as well aware as their critics of the wickedness of the Japanese." Avenging justice, too, plays an important role in the defense he makes of the postwar Nuremberg and Tokyo war crimes trials. These trials, he claims, fulfilled a vital moral task. The main trouble with the Kellogg Pact and the policy of nonrecognition and moral sanctions, according to Stimson, was that they named the international lawbreakers but failed to capture and punish them. The United States, along with other nations in the prewar world, had neglected "a duty to catch the criminal. . . . Our offense was thus that of the man who passed by on the other side." Now, this is a curious revision of the parable of the Good Samaritan, to which the Secretary here alludes. According to the Stimson version, the Good Samaritan should not have stopped to bind up the victim's wounds, put him on his beast of burden, and arrange for his care. Had he been cognizant of his real moral duty, he would rather have mounted his steed and rode off in hot pursuit of the robbers, to bring them to justice. This is only an illustration, but an apt one, of the prevailing concept of America's moral duty, with its emphasis on meting out justice rather than doing good (Stimson and Bundy, *On Active Service*, 384, 262).

tion of America's moral task played in the formulation of the American war aims in the Far East, with their twin goals of unconditional surrender and the destruction of Japan as a major power, especially after the desire to vindicate American principles and to punish the aggressor was intensified a hundredfold by the attack on Pearl Harbor.[23] To pursue the later implications of this kind of morality in foreign policy, with its attendant legalistic and vindictive overtones, would, however, be a task for another volume.

In contrast, the different kind of policy which Grew advocated and toward which Roosevelt so long inclined need not really be considered immoral or unprincipled, however much it undoubtedly would have been denounced as such. A limited *modus vivendi* agreement would not have required the United States in any way to sanction Japanese aggression or to abandon her stand on Chinese integrity and independence. It would have constituted only a recognition that the American government was not then in a position to enforce its principles, reserving for America full freedom of action at some later, more favorable time. Nor would it have meant the abandonment and betrayal of China. Rather it would have involved the frank recognition that the kind of help the Chinese wanted was impossible for the United States to give at that time. It would in no way have precluded giving China the best kind of help then possible—in the author's opinion, the offer of American mediation for a truce in the war and the grant of fuller economic aid to try to help the Chinese

recover—and promising China greater assistance once the crucial European situation was settled. Only that kind of morality which sees every sort of dealing with an aggressor, every instance of accommodation or conciliation, as appeasement and therefore criminal would find the policy immoral.[24]

What the practical results of such a policy, if attempted, would have been is of course a matter for conjecture. It would be rash to claim that it would have saved China, either from her wartime collapse or from the final victory of communism. It may well be that already in 1941 the situation in China was out of control. Nor can one assert with confidence that, had this policy enabled her to keep out of war with Japan, the United States would have been able to bring greater forces to bear in Europe much earlier, thus shortening the war and saving more of Europe from communism. Since the major part of the American armed forces were always concentrated in Europe and since in any case a certain proportion would have had to stand guard in the Pacific, it is possible that the avoidance of war with Japan, however desirable in itself, would not have made a decisive difference in the duration of the European conflict. The writer does, however, permit himself the modest conclusions that the kind of policy advocated by Grew presented real possibilities of success entirely closed to the policy actually followed and that it was by no means so immoral and unprincipled that it could not have been pursued by the United States with decency and honor.

[23] Admiral William D. Leahy (*I Was There* [New York: McGraw-Hill, 1950], 81) expresses his view of America's war aims in dubious Latin but with admirable forthrightness: "*Delenda est Japanico.*" He was, of course, not the only American leader to want to emulate Cato.

[24] See the introductory remarks on the possibilities of appeasement, under certain circumstances, as a useful diplomatic tool, along with an excellent case study in the wrong use of it, in J. W. Wheeler-Bennett, *Munich: Prologue to Tragedy* (London: Macmillan, 1948), 3–8.

Suggestions for Additional Reading

No American historian has yet tabulated the books and articles dealing with foreign affairs, the debates in the *Congressional Record,* or the discussions in public forums and over the radio by which the impact on the American people might be measured as war clouds gathered over Europe and Asia in the decade before the Japanese struck at Pearl Harbor. But from the outbreak of war in Europe in 1939, and particularly after the *Blitzkrieg* of the spring of 1940, a "Great Debate" engaged Congress, the press, and the public over the extent to which the United States should concern herself with affairs elsewhere in the world. The student will not find any sizable collection of the arguments of "isolationists" and "interventionists" gathered together, but must search for them in the press and the *Congressional Record.*

The surprise attack put a momentary stop to the debate, but it was almost immediately perceived that the issue of who was to blame for the disaster at Pearl Harbor implied judgments about Roosevelt's whole foreign policy in the years before war came. Both those supporting the administration and those who questioned its policy set in motion investigations to establish the facts. The requirements of wartime security prevented many of the details from becoming public during the first years of the war, but eventually a great mass of testimony was made available in the forty-odd volumes of the *Report* of the Joint Congressional Committee on Pearl Harbor, including both the majority and minority reports. Two convenient collections of excerpts from such testimony are Hans Louis Trefousse, editor, *What Happened at Pearl Harbor* (New York, 1958) and Paul S. Burtness and Warren U. Ober, editors, *The Puzzle of Pearl Harbor* (Evanston, Illinois, 1962).

As official archives have been opened, the records of enemy countries made available, and the diaries and memoirs of those concerned with America's foreign relations published, historians in generous number have developed their interpretations of what happened. The student in search of facts or opinions will find no dearth of material. The selections included in the foregoing readings are centered for the most part directly on the two issues, the relations of the United States and Japan and the blame for the surprise attack. Limitations of space make it necessary to omit much pertinent detail in the arguments of the authors. Consequently further reading in the books from which selections have been taken is recommended. A notable review article by Louis Morton, "Pearl Harbor in Perspective, A Bibliographical Survey," may be found in the *United States Naval Institute Proceedings,* Vol. 81, No. 4, April, 1955.

One of the best of the early efforts to acquaint the reader with the developments that led to war was *How War Came* (New York, 1942) by Forrest Davis and Ernest K. Lindley, two able journalists. Walter Millis in *This Is Pearl* (New York, 1947) has woven a highly readable account of the fateful and inexorable movement of events down to December 7 which leaves most of the blame for the disaster resting on the island commanders. Other works centered on the limited subject of culpability for the military and naval defeat are articles by General Sherman Miles, "Pearl Harbor in Retrospect," *Atlantic Monthly*, July, 1948, by Captain Tracy B. Kittredge, U.S.N.R., ret., "United States Defense Policy and Strategy; 1941," in *U.S. News and World Report*, December 3, 1954, and by Colonel T. N. Dupuy, "Pearl Harbor: Who Blundered?" in *American Heritage*, Vol. 13, No. 2, February 1962.

In his volume on the history of the Navy in World War II, *The Rising Sun in the Pacific* (Boston, 1948), Samuel Eliot Morison devotes the opening chapters to an analysis of Japanese policy in the Far East, attempting a balanced assessment of the factors in the surprise attack. The same area is covered by Mark S. Watson, *Chief of Staff: Prewar Plans and Preparations, United States Army in World War II* (Washington, 1950).

In a more general discussion of the administration of American foreign policy, the point of view favorable to Roosevelt found in the selections from Feis and Rauch is supplemented by John Gunther's *Roosevelt in Retrospect* (New York, 1950), a readable but superficial account. The most substantial work is the thorough examination of policy undertaken by William L. Langer and S. Everett Gleason, *The Challenge to Isolation, 1937–1940* (New York, 1952) and *The Undeclared War, 1940–1941* (New York, 1953). Langer and Gleason conclude that Roosevelt and Hull did not desire to lead the United States into war. They hold that Roosevelt lagged behind public opinion in moving toward partici-

pation in the world conflict, although they present evidence for the argument that the administration of foreign policy was often carelessly handled. More briefly, articles by Herbert Feis in *The Yale Review*, March, 1956, and Dexter Perkins in *The Virginia Quarterly Review*, Summer, 1954, sum up the arguments favorable to the Administration's conduct of affairs.

On the other side, in addition to the selections from Chamberlin, Tansill, and Beard in this volume, the case against Roosevelt and his advisers is argued emphatically in George Morgenstern, *Pearl Harbor: The Story of the Secret War* (New York, 1947), which accuses Roosevelt of secretly maneuvering a reluctant America into an unnecessary war by means of devious and unconstitutional methods. Frederick C. Sanborn, a specialist in international law, subjects the Administration's moves to close examination, testing what was said with what was done, in his *Design for War: A Study of Secret Power Politics* (New York, 1951). John T. Flynn, *The Roosevelt Myth* (New York, 1948), contends that Roosevelt sought war to save his political position.

The student may well want to read several lively articles which support or attack some of the above-mentioned books. One, by Samuel Eliot Morison, is a critical review of Beard's work, "Did Roosevelt Start the War—History through a Beard," *Atlantic Monthly*, August, 1948. Another, also highly critical of the revisionists, is Arthur M. Schlesinger, Jr., "Roosevelt and His Detractors," *Harper's Magazine*, June, 1950. Four others, available in pamphlet form, were written by Harry Elmer Barnes in support of the revisionist writings of Beard, Morgenstern, Sanborn, Tansill, and Chamberlin: *The Struggle against the*

Historical Blackout (ninth, revised, enlarged edition, no date), *Was Roosevelt Pushed into War by Popular Demand in 1941?*, a caveat against a paper read by Dexter Perkins at the 1950 meeting of the American Historical Association, *Rauch on Roosevelt*, which attacks Rauch's interpretations and impugns him as an historian, and *The Court Historians versus Revisionism*, in which Barnes assails the volume by Langer and Gleason. Finally, for the revisionists, Barnes has edited a symposium, *Perpetual War for Perpetual Peace* (Caldwell, Idaho, 1953), which includes the article by William L. Neumann, "How American Policy Toward Japan Contributed to War in the Pacific."

Works which furnish important background on our foreign policy are A. Whitney Griswold, *The Far Eastern Policy of the United States* (New York, 1938), George F. Kennan's *American Diplomacy 1900–1950* (Chicago, 1951), Foster Rhea Dulles, *America's Rise to World Power, 1898–1954* (New York, 1954) and two works on the Japanese policy, David J. Lu, *From the Marco Polo Bridge to Pearl Harbor; Japan's Entry into World War II* (New York, 1961), and Robert J. C. Butow, *Tojo and the Coming of the War* (Princeton, 1961). Joseph W. Ballantine, who worked at the side of Cordell Hull during the difficult negotiations before the war, has provided his view in "Mukden to Pearl Harbor," *Foreign Affairs*, July, 1949.

Equipped with the knowledge of events and with the arguments before him the reader may want to explore the writings of some of the participants and judge their motives for himself. In *The Memoirs of Cordell Hull* (New York, 1948) and in *On Active Service* by Henry L. Stimson and McGeorge Bundy (New York, 1948) two of the Administration's leaders tell their story. Much of value may be found in Robert E. Sherwood's *Roosevelt and Hopkins* (New York, 1948) since Sherwood was close to both men and has drawn heavily from records they left. Of others, Joseph C. Grew's *Ten Years in Japan* (New York, 1944) and the account by a Japanese liberal, Toshikazu Kase, *Journey to the Missouri* (New Haven, 1950) are especially appropriate.

The Public Papers and Addresses of Franklin Delano Roosevelt, edited by Judge Samuel I. Rosenman, contain in Volume X much material of value for the problem. The viewpoint of the British government is provided in Sir Llewellyn Woodward, *British Foreign Policy in the Second World War* (London, 1962) and in the words of Britain's great leader Winston S. Churchill in *The Grand Alliance* (Boston, 1950), Vol. 3 of his account of the war.